Best Ideas From America's Blue Ribbon Schools

A joint publication of
The National Association of Elementary School Principals
and
Corwin Press, Inc.

Best Ideas From America's Blue Ribbon Schools

What Award-Winning Elementary and Middle School Principals Do

National Association of Elementary School Principals

NAESP

CORWIN PRESS, INC.
A Sage Publications Company
Thousand Oaks, California

PHOTO CREDITS: The Advent School, Boston, MA; Christa McAuliffe Elementary, Lewisville, TX; Fay School, Southborough, MA; Northeast School, Monroe Township, NJ; Show Low Primary School, Show Low, AZ; Southwest Elementary, Howell, MI.

For information address:

Corwin Press, Inc.
A Sage Publications Company
2455 Teller Road
Thousand Oaks, California 91320

SAGE Publications Ltd.
6 Bonhill Street
London EC2A 4PU
United Kingdom

SAGE Publications India Pvt. Ltd.
M-32 Market
Greater Kailash I
New Delhi 110 048 India

Printed in the United States of America

Library of Congress Cataloging-in-Publication Data

Best ideas from America's blue ribbon schools : what award-winning
    elementary and middle-school principals do.
        p. cm.
    ISBN 0–8039–6177–4
    1. Elementary school administration—United States. 2. Elementary
school principals—United States. 3. Middle School administration—
United States. 4. Middle school principals—United States. I. National
Association of Elementary School Principals (U.S.)
LB2822.5.N25   1994
372.12'00973—dc20   94–2934

94 95 96 97 98 10 9 8 7 6 5 4 3 2 1

Corwin Press Production Editor: Marie Louise Penchoen

Contents

 Foreword

Recently, the Department of Education released a report entitled "Youth Indicators for 1993, Trends in the Well-Being of American Youth." It is an impressive document that spotlights the lives of our children in 1993. Three ideas from this report deserve special mention.

First, in the past 10 years there has been a quantum leap in the educational aspirations of our young people. Our children know that the world is changing and that a good education remains their best chance to make it in today's society. They are getting the message that you are not born smart but that you get smart by stretching your mind. This is all to the good and suggests that schools that set new standards for excellence will increasingly get a positive response from students and parents.

Second, the report reveals that young people still place a great value on the role and the influence of their parents in shaping their lives. Despite television, video games, and peer pressure, parents still have a powerful capacity to shape the lives of their children for the better by setting high standards. This suggests that schools need to find new ways to help parents slow down their lives in order to help their children grow. Fortunately, as this report indicates, many of America's finest schools are already headed in that direction.

Third, if we Americans want to compete in the global economy, we are going to have to give up being comfortable with just being average. American education needs to respond to the fundamental changes in the global economy and to recognize that now is the time to establish a world-class standard of education for every child. This is the reason why the push by so many good schools to strengthen their curriculum is so important and heartening.

Now, some people tell me that the problem with trying to achieve excellence is that you cannot really do it for all of our children—it will not be equitable, and kids at the bottom will just sink even further behind. My response to this thinking is that excellence and equality are not incompatible; we have just never tried hard enough in this country to achieve them both for all of our children. This is particularly true when it comes to providing an education to our disadvantaged children who sometimes have the whole world stacked against them. The last thing they need is a watered-down curriculum.

This is why we are pushing hard to create voluntary national standards of academic excellence—a commitment to a world-class education for every child. Creating the context for a world-class education for every child is what the Blue Ribbon Schools do every day. As you read through this stimulating collection, you will see that these schools have a talent for reaching for high standards in many different ways. This is how it should be.

The many fine contributions from these Blue Ribbon Schools tell us that the best American educators already have a keen sense of what must be done to prepare our children for the coming times. These "best ideas" from these wonderful schools give a clear indication of what it takes to reach for excellence: (a) a sense of shared purpose among faculty, students, parents, and the wider community; (b) an environment that conveys the message that all children can learn; (c) a spirit of innovation and the clear recognition that schools have to change to remain as good as they are; (d) a strong commitment to character development and values; (e) an ongoing program of student assessment and school improvement; and (f) a constant striving for academic excellence.

It is my sincere hope that parents, teachers, and the many fine Americans who are dedicating their lives to the education of this nation's children will find these wonderful suggestions a stimulating source of information and inspiration.

Richard W. Riley
U.S. Secretary of Education

# Introduction

The very best schools are learning communities, with a commitment to education that extends not only to all the children but also to all the adults in the building. Among the most creative leaders of these learning communities are the principals of elementary and middle schools that have been selected as "Blue Ribbon Schools" by the U.S. Department of Education. Their designation as "blue-ribbon" winners says it all—these schools have demonstrated an unusual ability to create an atmosphere that promotes learning for *everyone*.

When the elementary and middle school principals of the 1991-1992 award-winning schools met in Washington, DC, we asked them to share a "best idea" that they had put into practice in their schools. The National Association of Elementary School Principals (NAESP) received over 100 submissions in a variety of categories. From these, a panel of principals and editors selected new or unique ideas that were both appropriate for designated categories and provided sufficient information on the benefits for children, schools, and communities.

I hasten to point out that the categories for these best ideas are somewhat arbitrary. You will find, for example, that ideas in the "technology" section also enrich the "curriculum" section; activities that enhance "critical-thinking skills" also affect the "school improvement/restructuring process."

The final section, "Even More 'Best Ideas!'," contains a potpourri of exciting ideas that did not have enough counterparts to form an entire section. Nonetheless, each is a gem in itself.

What follows is a smorgasbord of fascinating ideas that elementary and middle schools across America can use and adapt to make education a more enriching experience for everyone. I hope you will use these best ideas as you continue to work on creating an outstanding learning community in your school.

Samuel G. Sava
Executive Director
National Association of Elementary School Principals

Reading and discussing books.

Strengthening Curriculum Content

Helping young people develop skills and knowledge is a school's most important responsibility. This chapter includes examples of how Blue Ribbon Schools have made science, history, and literature come alive.

Learning is hard work, but it can also be exciting. In the best schools, there is electricity in the air as young minds explore, question, and learn. Imagine the excitement as history comes alive, and students milk a cow, shear a sheep, or learn how to make a quilt. Or consider how a school's reading program could be improved if libraries were established in every classroom.

Blue Ribbon Schools have set high academic expectations for all their students. They find ways to challenge gifted, average, and at-risk students. Whether they are creating science immersion labs or sponsoring a "time machine" to teach research skills, these schools are finding ways to help every child succeed.

Science Immersion Labs

Description

Have you ever walked through a rain forest or experienced the chill of Antarctica?

Each semester, we select a schoolwide science theme, which then becomes the basis for creating a simulated environment. Each environment is enhanced with murals, sound effects, animals, and a variety of science experiment stations. These stations, led by volunteers, allow students to participate in hands-on science activities.

Benefits

The immersion labs give students the opportunity to learn vocabulary, to interpret maps, to analyze data, and to use scientific instruments. Teachers enrich the themes with appropriate literature, films, discussions, and related projects in each classroom.

The science immersion labs are always a highlight of the school year!

Dr. Bobbie Sferra, Principal
Sequoya Elementary School
Scottsdale, AZ

Mini-Libraries

Description

The results of a school-based survey indicated that the majority of our students would rather watch TV or play a game than read for pleasure. To change this preference, our school pursued a goal to increase leisure reading habits.

Through the joint efforts of the School Improvement Team and the faculty, mini-libraries were established in each classroom. Books were selected for their high-interest content, and children were encouraged to sample a variety of different ones. As an added incentive, children could get on the school's closed-circuit TV by writing book reviews and reading them for broadcast.

Benefits

Children's interest was increased, especially because we chose books that sparked their imaginations and excited them about reading. The process of reviewing books for broadcast enhanced a number of skills beyond reading—analytical thinking, writing, and speaking.

> Dolores B. Hardison, Principal
> Griffin Elementary School
> Cooper City, FL

World Fair and the Time Machine

Description

One of our best ideas has been to select a schoolwide theme for our yearly parent-student open house. For the past 2 years, we have focused on bringing the world into our classroom. Last year, each class completed a number of activities centered around a country they selected for a "World Fair." Classes displayed the country's flag on a bulletin board, did group research projects, wrote class informational books, and made child-sized pressboard dolls and dressed them in the authentic clothing of their selected country.

At the actual open house, ethnic meals were prepared, families placed pushpins on a world map indicating their original heritage, and passports were provided so that families could have them stamped as they "entered" each country.

This year's open house used various time periods. Each grade level represented a different period of time, and time lines were provided for each family as they walked through our "Time Machine."

Benefits

This idea has proven to be a successful way for us to make history come alive for our students. As they have learned through a variety of "relevant" activities, the children have become representatives of the country or time period they have studied. In addition, our parents have enthusiastically attended and participated in these activities.

Janet H. Brownlie, Elementary Principal
Adler Park School
Libertyville, IL

Literature Circles

Description

Over the past few years, we have moved to a very strong literature-based reading program. We have used money normally set aside for workbooks to purchase literature for our students. We have purchased multiple copies of many titles so that we may conduct "Literature Circles" in all of our grade levels.

Typically, we split a class into three groups of eight to nine students each. Parents, support staff, and/or the principal help out at such times, so that each group has an adult leader. Each group will read and discuss chapters of a book each day. Students will also complete, individually or in small groups, related written activities or research projects. At the end of the novel, conferences are held with individual students to share assessment of their contributions.

Benefits

The Literature Circles give all students an opportunity to participate in the discussion and in activities that are organized in relation to a particular book.

Duane L. Burns, Principal
Highland Elementary School
Apple Valley, MN

Texas Day

Description

Huffman Elementary has a large population of students new to Texas, as well as native Texan students who have little knowledge about their heritage. In response to this situation, staff and parents developed a schoolwide thematic unit called "Texas Day." Each year, this day brings the community together to help develop in children a knowledge and an appreciation for those people who settled this region.

Texas Day is filled with "being there" experiences. Everyone dresses in costume, and we have guest speakers who demonstrate quilt making, storytelling, milking (with a real cow), care of horses (with a real horse), sheepshearing (with a real sheep), honey collection (yes, with real beehives!), dancing the Cotton-eyed Joe, whistle making, saddle making, candle making, carving, and whittling. Other "guests" include a fangless rattlesnake, an alligator, and an armadillo.

Benefits

Besides the rich learning that takes place as a result of these real-life demonstrations, students can experience different environments. The entire school is transformed into simulations depicting old one-room schoolhouses, campfires, and old farmsteads. Texas Day culminates in an open-house celebration for the entire community, in which students share what they have learned and created.

Vicki Ann Halliday, Principal
Huffman Elementary School
Plano, TX

Red ribbons symbolize pride in being drug free.

Educating for Citizenship and Character

Thomas Jefferson believed that public schools played a critical role in preserving our nation's democracy. "An individual that hopes to be ignorant and free, hopes for something that never was and never will be," he once observed.

Today's Blue Ribbon Schools continue Jefferson's legacy. The projects described in this chapter illustrate some of the ways in which schools are shaping students' character and how they are preparing them to assume the responsibilities of citizenship.

Blue Ribbon Schools are teaching students important democratic values—a sense of responsibility, cooperation, hard work, patriotism, a love of the environment, generosity, self-respect, and courtesy are just a few. As students care for their school, take part in student government, or learn about positive behavior, they are learning lessons that will last a lifetime.

School Service Projects

Description

The concept of "School Service Projects" is gaining interest among our students. Children at all grade levels work in rotating teams and are given daily responsibilities.

Kindergartners regularly clean their own classrooms and even scrub the tables. First graders clear the lunch area after eating, in preparation for the upper grades. Second graders work on landscape projects and maintenance. Third graders help out in the library with tasks such as shelving books.

Fourth graders continually send squads out to wash windows around the school. Fifth graders tidy the lunch area after the upper grades finish eating. They also provide the ball room monitors and the school safety patrol.

Benefits

In the past, schools have often emphasized individual achievement and worth above service. We are demonstrating for our children the need to work in effective teams and to show commitment to an organization and to society. The School Service Projects are similar to those in Japan, where students are encouraged to work in teams to give service to their school.

Anthony W. Knight, Principal
Oak Hills Elementary School
Agoura, CA

Principal's Open Door

Description

Our principal has an "Open Door" policy on Fridays. Teachers select those who want to visit and share a piece of class work. Students of the Day or Week also are chosen to participate.

The principal spends a few minutes conversing with each child. Besides verbal praise, the children take away a "My Principal Loves Me" pen or pencil and an age-appropriate sticker. They also sign the guest register.

Benefits

We find that students who talk with our principal are likely to receive a boost to their self-esteem. In addition, they are able to see what is happening in other classes while they wait in line.

> Renée Lamkay, Principal
> Willow Elementary School
> Agoura Hills, CA

You Can Make a Difference

Description

Staff and students at our school select a theme to be used throughout the year. Our theme is advertised in school bulletins and newsletters and is used as a guide for selecting Students of the Week.

This year, the theme is "You Can Make a Difference." We chose complementary subthemes—"Get Organized," "Be Thankful for Small Things," "Give a Helping Hand," and "Resolve a Conflict in a Positive Way"—to help motivate us.

Twice a month, two students from each class are identified for their improvement or for a contribution they have made. Award winners are given recognition in class, a special pin, and a place of honor on the school bulletin board. We also congratulate their parents by letter.

Benefits

By using school themes, we are able to focus on social issues that lead to positive changes. For example, eight Boy Scout packs united to make a difference. They conducted a schoolwide cleanup that had dads on tractors, moms planting shrubs, and students putting down ground cover and bark.

In the same manner, our themes provide a way to attract business partnerships, which are proving to be helpful in promoting the needs of the school.

Joan M. Benbow, Principal
Alamo Elementary School
Alamo, CA

Exemplary Patriot

Description

Fourth through sixth graders are eligible to receive our school's most prestigious award, presented at semester-end programs honoring recipients. The criteria for earning the "Exemplary Patriot" award reflect a broad base having to do with participation, achievement, and service.

A student must accrue points in six distinct categories: (a) curricular, (b) school service, (c) cocurricular, (d) athletics, (e) leadership, and (f) effort and citizenship. Points are earned as the result of involvement or achievement in designated activities.

Benefits

The purpose of the Exemplary Patriot award is to recognize individuals who exemplify qualities we hope to foster in all students, such as (a) a desire for self-improvement, (b) dedication in reaching for goals, (c) service to others, and (d) willingness to be a positive role model.

To earn the Exemplary Patriot award, a student need not be a superstar. He or she must be an active and enthusiastic member of our school, engaged in the pursuit of excellence, and able to meet certain standards of performance.

Janet L. Young, Principal
Fort Washington Elementary School
Fresno, CA

Student Council

Description

Our "Student Council" is a reflection of the school's philosophical ideal—character development.

Each month, fourth through sixth graders are evaluated numerically from 1 to 4 on industry, courtesy, responsibility, and scholarship. Individuals whose monthly average is 4 in the first three areas are on the council for that month.

We feel that the scholarship rating, by itself, should not affect eligibility. If students are performing at their best in the first three qualities, they are also at their strongest academically.

Benefits

At our school, the Student Council is a testimony that character development goes hand in hand with academic and personal growth. We find that by upholding the above standards for membership, we accomplish the goal of creating a model for all students as well as offering service to our school and the community.

Dr. Joan Lutton, Headmistress
Cheryl Rogers, Elementary Principal
The Cushman School
Miami, FL

Junior Naturalists

Description

Awareness of the environment is a way of life on our semitropical island. We integrate the study of the earth into the entire curriculum, providing students with a number of ways to appreciate and care for their surroundings.

For example, the "Junior Naturalist" program trains fifth graders as tour guides for children visiting a nearby national wildlife refuge. In addition, students are invited to join in the annual coastal cleanup drive to rid the beaches of harmful debris.

At the Shell Show, fifth graders inform visitors about live shells and other marine life in their aquariums. All classes are able to observe nature, collect shells, and draw sketches on various beach trips.

The Environmental Committee promotes awareness of the importance of recycling and conservation. Two representatives from each room meet regularly with the principal to discuss their concerns and ideas. They recently aided in the planting of a hardwood hammock on campus.

Benefits

The programs we offer encourage students to value the beauty and the uniqueness of their environment. By organizing a variety of projects, assemblies, field trips, and workdays, we help them take responsibility for the care of the earth.

Barbara T. Ward, Principal
Sanibel Elementary School
Sanibel, FL

Citizenship and Giving

Description

Giving of oneself is an attitude and a way of life we aim to develop; this year, we supported a multitude of projects that contributed both to school and to community.

Second graders visited the elderly. Fourth graders comprised the Bingo Brigade, entertaining residents of a local care center. Fifth and sixth graders made Valentine's Day care packages to take to the Veterans Hospital. In addition, a number of our students are involved in a peace project that donated garage sale income to an environmental association.

Christmas was a special time of giving for everyone on campus. The less fortunate received donated food and clothing, and students served at a free lunch program. Live-action scenes were created in classroom windows for our gift to the community, an old-fashioned Christmas walk.

Sixth graders learned about citizenship while conducting a campaign to elect Student Council officers. During the year, the council held meetings every other week, offered school tours, and prepared for emergencies in cooperation with local optimist clubs. Members also promoted good school citizenship by doing "Polite People" presentations.

Benefits

Honesty, devotion, discipline, and responsibility are reinforced at our school. We uphold the Golden Rule and applaud those who care about their school, city, state, and world community.

Raymond J. Pechous, Principal
Regina Elementary School
Iowa City, IA

Word of the Week

Description

We have devised a responsibility plan as a way of helping students learn to be more accountable for their actions. One part of the plan includes a "Word of the Week."

Each Monday, a special word is presented and defined during morning announcements. On other days of the week, all students hear the word in a sentence, learn its synonym, and discover how the word translates into everyday situations. For example, it might be mentioned that "Mrs. Brown's students were very *responsible* when they picked up litter at recess."

Sample words include *organized, effort, friendly,* and *cooperative.* The Word of the Week is prominently displayed throughout the school.

Benefits

The Word of the Week is a positive way of encouraging and teaching positive behavior at school. Parents are asked to follow up at home as well.

Doug Harris, Principal
Leawood Elementary School
Leawood, KS

Character Development

Description

A newly implemented "Character Development" policy reflects our commitment to cultivating good citizens. We have a program that teaches 15 core values such as responsibility, honesty, freedom, equality, justice, abstinence, respect for self, and caring for others.

Monthly themes encourage basic personal, social, and civic values. Classroom teachers and our counselor integrate the themes into the curriculum, giving students ample opportunity to practice positive qualities.

Our Character Development policy is written and updated as a joint effort of students and teachers. Pupils are responsible for their own class assignments, work areas, and homework. They share in keeping the building clean, maintain their own schedules, and move freely to special activities without direct supervision.

As outreach to others, the Student Council participates in a food drive, a holiday hat-and-mitten tree, the multiple sclerosis "read-a-thon," and visits to local nursing homes. Classrooms are paired to plan cooperative activities throughout the year. For example, sixth graders serve as helpers in kindergarten, and student buddies are selected to welcome new students.

Benefits

Our citizenship program is a success, in part, because staff members continually model the essence of a democratic society. Starting in kindergarten, classes discuss appropriate behavior and how to get along with others. Teachers regularly make introductory telephone calls to all parents, send home "good news" postcards, and implement cooperative learning techniques.

Likewise, administrators make weekly calls to share with parents, write positive comments on report cards, give quarterly citizenship awards, and select a Bus Citizen of the Month.

Jill M. Ramsey, Principal
River Bend Elementary School
Chesterfield, MO

Youth Service Learning

Description

Our students learn about helping others and giving back to the community through "Youth Service Learning" projects. Each classroom identifies a service recipient, such as the Ronald McDonald House or the Senior Center. Although the project itself is important, the best discoveries occur when students *reflect* on their experiences through discussion groups and written activities.

Teachers encourage students to choose projects that integrate into the existing curriculum. This year, first graders investigated the research process by studying bears. They bought stuffed bears for a children's home; the money ($1,200) was collected from pledges for running the mile in physical education class. All 175 students posed for a group photo with the bears. Later, the director of the home became the guest speaker for the class.

Benefits

The Youth Service Learning program provides excellent training for situations that our students might meet beyond the classroom. We have not only educated and enlightened our young people but we have also made possible valuable exchanges with the entire community.

Linda S. Saukkonen, Principal
Clear Springs Elementary School
Minnetonka, MN

Hero's Day

Description

Our school hosts an annual "Hero's Day" fair, the culmination of an in-depth schoolwide exploration of heroism—famous heroes, heroes in our community, heroes in our family, and the hero within each of us.

On Hero's Day, we demonstrate interdisciplinary teaching and learning at its finest. Social studies, language arts, fine arts, science, math, and computer technology are all called into play.

We can also combine this unit with our marking of Holocaust Day, at which time we plan speakers, films, and readings of relevant literature.

Benefits

During Hero's Day activities, we learn and share with community members, parents, and visiting students. Most important to all of us, however, are the character and value "lessons" appropriated by the students. Pre- and postunit surveys attest to the heightened standards and sensitivities on campus as a result of the heroism program.

Rabbi Yonah Fuld, Principal
Audrey G. Schurgin, Associate Principal
Salanter Akiba Riverdale Academy
Riverdale, NY

Troubleshooters and Mediators

Description

Selected students in our fifth and sixth grades have received training in the skills of conflict management. Students wearing a special sash on campus are peer mediators, known as "troubleshooters" and "conflict managers."

When students experience disagreements between one another, they are scheduled into sessions with a pair of mediators who help them "clear the air." The mediators monitor the verbal interaction of the disagreeing students. They also help those in conflict set mutually agreed-on goals to resolve differences. Once there is cooperation, the students may rejoin their classmates on the playground, in class, or in the cafeteria.

Benefits

Conflict management education has been positive for our entire student body. Many students aspire to be mediators, and others respond favorably to peer intervention.

Dr. Catherine P. Swami, Principal
Kilgour Elementary School
Cincinnati, OH

Social Skills Recess

Description

Our staff teaches, models, and practices all school rules and expectations for both new and returning students. If a student chooses not to follow a rule, has an unresolved conflict, or acts in an unsafe manner, a staff member may assign that person to "Social Skills Recess," a special 30-minute session held during the student's lunch period. This guarantees that no classroom teaching time is lost.

This recess is facilitated by the physical education instructor as part of the regularly scheduled working day. Our counselor prepares this teacher with the necessary skills to lead students toward good choices.

Assigned students meet in the gym with five to six other children. By working in small groups, they can role-play actions that were inappropriate and then practice more acceptable alternatives. They help each other act out all kinds of different situations. During this time, playground games are taught to those who are too timid to join in.

Benefits

The Social Skills Recess is one of our best ideas, a proven winner in reducing playground confrontations and in enhancing student self-esteem.

Helen B. Patton, Principal
Slater/Filmore Grade School
Burns, OR

Volunteers for the Multiply Impaired

Description

We have many students who volunteer to assist the multiply impaired and deaf children on our campus. On a regular basis, volunteers interact with our unusually large population of pupils who require help with motor skills, class assignments, and even routine communication. The volunteers share games, read stories, and involve themselves in activities on behalf of their classmates who need them.

Sign language is available for hearing students who want to open communication among their peers. The school honors outstanding volunteers each month and also gives them an end-of-the-year salute.

Benefits

Even without spoken language, children forge bonds of friendship through smiles and touches. The positive experiences of our volunteers transfer to academics, becoming the foundation for writing projects and discussions.

Meredith Wedin, Principal
T. H. Rogers School
Houston, TX

School Family

Description

We have created a "School Family" as a way to keep up the spirits of seventh and eighth graders in a school that also has kindergartners. This makes it possible for all to lead, not just those elected to the Student Council.

Our entire school is divided into families. Two to three students from each grade, along with a staff member, act as the head of a family.

Each month, we gather for "family" led by an eighth-grade family member. Eighth graders have planned school projects in class and are ready to lead. Examples of different activities are: creating a family song; decorating doors for a holiday; leading field, board, and community-building games; and discussing honesty, respect, and other such topics.

Benefits

Every student gets a chance to lead along with an eighth-grade partner. We have noticed that the family concept helps students get acquainted with others from different classes. It has really helped to lessen fear of the "big kids" by the younger students.

Karen Tarabochia, Principal
St. Philomena Catholic School
Des Moines, WA

Discovering together.

3 Implementing Cooperative Learning

One of the most important lessons students need to learn in school is how to work with others as part of a team. From self-managing teams in factories to scientific research teams seeking the cure for many diseases, today's workplace requires that people know how to work together; so does today's society. Students who learn how to respect and get along with a wide variety of other students in school will be better able to adapt to an increasingly diverse world.

Blue Ribbon Schools are fostering the collaborative process among students *and* teachers. This chapter includes several examples of ways in which these excellent schools have increased cooperation and improved education for all children.

The Bagel Breakfast Bunch

Description

Our teachers are enthusiastic about a breakfast idea hosted by the principal. We all gather for a 30-minute before-school session to share coffee/bagels/cream cheese and creative uses for cooperative learning.

Once a month, our principal facilitates this optional meeting where teachers may ask one question or offer one good idea. We write down our ideas beforehand, if possible, for easy note taking.

Almost half the staff showed up the first three times. As a result of requests for extended training, we also are planning 2-hour Monday evening box suppers where participants will receive professional development credits. Several staff members, who have had advanced training, now are able to lead the others.

Benefits

The breakfast idea really works! Even elementary teachers have heard about it and have asked to come.

The key seems to be the exchange of practical applications that teachers learn from each other. Everyone can participate. We receive at least one or two new ideas to bring about a quick response in our classrooms.

Carole H. Iwanicki, Principal
Mansfield Middle School
Storrs, CT

Choices for the Gifted

Description

Our gifted program is based on the belief that all children have talents and interests that need to be nurtured. The curriculum model we use allows a choice of learning alternatives for a portion of the school day.

Each semester, parents assist their children in selecting four to six classes from a smorgasbord of electives. Students may match their interests and talents with a wide variety of courses, including visual and performing arts, technology, special-content topics in basic subject areas, foreign languages, citizenship, and sports.

The most popular elective, Circle of Learning, gives children of differing ages an opportunity to work together. Under the direction of a supervising teacher, older students meet with primary-level youngsters on a one-to-one basis in the areas of language arts, reading, and math.

Benefits

Our gifted program provides students with an array of choices for growth. As a result of the Circle of Learning, for example, both older and younger students have experienced gains in academic achievement, social acceptance, responsibility, and self-confidence. Many lasting multi-age friendships have been formed, and students have shown significant progress in their total development.

Joyce Faulkner, Principal
Lewis H. Powell Gifted and Talented Magnet
Elementary School
Raleigh, NC

Intracollaborative Hour

Description

The "Intracollaborative Hour" began as a way to integrate a self-contained gifted room with "regular ed" students and has since expanded to include all four classes of each grade.

Students, who are at the same grade level but of differing academic abilities, work in small groups on a nonacademic project 1 hour each week. By meeting with two or three others who are not in their own classrooms, they all become better acquainted.

A team of teachers plans the activities and determines how students from each room will participate. This year, projects have varied from murals to interview biographies, and from favors for a nursing home to original skits and plays. We are planning activities for the future that will focus on conflict resolution.

Benefits

Both students and teachers are benefiting from this special hour. The interchanges have encouraged new friendships; the cross-class groupings are seen especially at recess. Providing the opportunity for more children to know one another better also has reduced conflicts and problems that would otherwise come to the office.

Teachers are collaborating as well. Over the summer they pulled together units, lessons, and materials from many sources in preparation for a friendly, peaceful year.

Linda Ward, Principal
Pine Elementry School
North Olmsted, OH

Cooperating Across the Curriculum

Description

Cooperative learning lends itself greatly to teaching across the curriculum. We are inspired by the beneficial results we have achieved by integrating math, science, social studies, and language arts in the classroom.

The second-grade teacher has used cooperative learning effectively in creative drama and poetry activities to enrich science, social studies, literature, and even math programs. Students are given a safety net in which they can dare to be creative in front of their peers. They write their own plays, raps, and poems, some complete with sound effects and lighting. (Camping flashlights make great floodlights!)

Benefits

Cooperative learning is the key ingredient of an exciting atmosphere conducive to learning. When children are able to brainstorm and to collaborate in a nonthreatening situation, there is a high level of enthusiasm, and instruction is consequently reinforced.

Dr. Annette C. Smith, Principal
Charlotte Lawler, Second-Grade Teacher
Good Shepherd Episcopal School
Dallas, TX

Helping *all* students achieve success.

Helping At-Risk Students and Preventing Dropout

Blue Ribbon Schools are committed to helping *all* students achieve success. They have developed a variety of programs to meet the needs of students who are at risk of school failure.

Early intervention is critical for these students. If the United States is to meet National Education Goal 2—that the high school graduation rate will increase to at the least 90% by the Year 2000—we cannot wait until students reach high school before intervening. The elementary school programs outlined in this chapter *are* setting at-risk youngsters on the path to school success.

Today's children face a variety of problems, including poverty and the disintegration of the typical family structure. Schools cannot solve these problems by themselves. That is why so many of the programs outlined in this chapter involve partnerships with the community.

Demographers suggest that the number of children at risk in the United States is increasing. Programs such as these can help ensure that all our nation's children acquire the skills and the knowledge that they will need as they enter the 21st century.

Friday Kids

Description

Our special-services teacher developed the "Friday Kids" program to give extra academic assistance to students in the first through the sixth grades who are struggling and in danger of becoming at risk.

Children who are not already in the special-services program are recommended by their classroom teachers to be Friday Kids. Once a week, they meet with the special-services teacher and her aide to work in areas where they need additional help. Two grades are chosen to participate during each quarter, rotating through all the grades.

Benefits

Feedback from staff, parents, and, especially, our children indicates that the Friday Kids program has made a significant difference in students' progress and in their self-esteem! We feel that we are successful in preventing an increase in those who are at risk.

Steven L. Duke, Principal
Quailwood Elementary School
Bakersfield, CA

Drug-Free Dog

Description

Each year, we plan a "Drug and Alcohol Free" program with the special assistance of our fifth-grade students and with funds from the Parent/Teacher Organization and a Youth Resources grant. We hold the program at four sites on the same night to serve four different neighborhood communities.

Children receive free T-shirts, all the pizza they can eat, and soft drinks. The hit of the evening is the state police drug dog, who helps officers put on a 20-minute educational program. For more fun, the fifth graders have arranged games and prizes for everyone.

All local preschoolers, age three to five, also are invited to have a good time with us while learning how to be drug free. We design a new shirt every year and give away over 700 T-shirts on party night.

Benefits

We get excellent comments from parents about the Drug and Alcohol Free program. They especially appreciate that we come to the communities where the children live.

James H. Kolb, Principal
Brumfield Elementary School
Princeton, IN

Back on Track

Description

We offer an alternative school program designed for over-age students going into the seventh grade who want to get back "on track" with their peers.

Our staff selects students to take language arts, social studies, math, and science in their last year at the middle school. During the year, the young people are also transported to the high school to attend two electives.

The program provides an accelerated-skills curriculum after which successful students are promoted to the ninth grade, bypassing 1 year at the middle school.

Benefits

The alternative program works very well at getting kids back on track and at grade level. We purposefully have avoided creating a "watered-down" curriculum so that motivated students have a solid opportunity to catch up.

Mary Sue Ward, Principal
Thomas B. Bryan and Larry Hunt, Former Principals
Cook Middle School
Adel, GA

A Sense of Belonging

Description

We have developed a coordinated program to involve students in our educational community. We feel that a sense of belonging is especially vital to the at-risk student's success.

We teach conflict resolution in all classes. Trained students become conflict managers on the playground. In addition, older students act as tutors to younger students, and every class has a "Buddy Class" for special learning activities.

All sixth graders have regular jobs on campus. Examples include Principal's Assistant, Safety Patrol Officer, and Kindergarten Reader. The Student Council coordinates its goals with the school goals and acts as an advisory council for school decisions.

Benefits

By establishing a coordinated program, we have made an effort to help children, especially those who are at risk, feel a sense of ownership in our school. Giving students an important role to play helps ensure that students feel they belong and are important members of our educational community.

Penny F. Heim, Principal
Indian Creek Elementary School
Olathe, KS

Support One Student

Description

Our school supports at-risk students with two successful programs that match students with teachers who volunteer to serve as mentors.

In the "Support One Student" program, at-risk students help tutor other students in the mentor teacher's classroom, stay after school to perform housekeeping activities, eat lunch with the mentor, and sometimes attend a social function, such as a school sports event, for an extra-special time together.

In our after-school tutoring program, four to five pupils meet with each of 10 volunteer teachers who assist with homework twice a week. First, students receive a snack and then study with the tutors for 1 hour. Parents are also invited to come and learn how to work with their children on schoolwork. This program is funded by an at-risk grant.

Benefits

Our mentors and tutors are building positive ongoing relationships with at-risk students and their parents. Attendance and motivation have been at a constant high, and year-end evaluations show our success in providing students with positive attention and academic support.

Earl Martin, Principal
Countryside Elementary School
Olathe, KS

Programs for the At-Risk Child

Description

Our school has a range of programs that help connect the at-risk child and the family to the school.

"Safe Start" provides a warm, supervised place for students to gather before the school day begins. Corporate sponsorship pays a parent coordinator, and other parents volunteer their time.

"New Kids on the Block" puts a focus on children who enter classes during the year. Initial contact is made through the guidance counselor, with student buddies and peer interaction serving as team components.

"Homework Helpers," funded by corporate sponsors, provides daily, after-school assisted support for children in Grades 3 through 5. Students may also ask for help with how to use the library and media resources.

Our school has an "Assistance Team"—administrator, nurse, teacher, social worker, and learning specialists—to review weekly teacher referrals and to develop a coordinated plan of action. This team is not a part of the formalized special education plan.

We also are fortunate to have a "Connection Team," a group of three professionals who focus on individual families. A teacher, a nurse, and a social worker work with the school-age child, any younger children, and their family to build positive connections.

Benefits

Students at risk need continuous, specialized attention and support to have a chance to use the best that schools have to offer. With our comprehensive programs, we are able to provide these children with an additional boost when we feel it is needed.

Miriam L. Remar, Principal
Howard C. Reiche Community School
Portland, ME

First-Grade Intervention

Description

During the first 2 weeks of school, we identify incoming first graders who require supportive services by using a combination of kindergarten teachers' recommendations and testing results.

The intervention teacher gathers all pertinent data to design a specific program for those who need extra help. There are meetings with prior teachers; if possible, conferences with the reading specialist; and times to get acquainted with the student to establish a good working relationship.

Children in our program spend time with the intervention teacher, on a one-to-one basis, for approximately 20 minutes a day. These intensive, task-oriented sessions occur in addition to regular classroom instruction.

Benefits

For the past 5 years, we have used this intervention system to identify and assist first-grade students who are at risk. During the school year, evaluations are conducted by the intervention teacher, the classroom teacher, the reading specialist, and the principal to determine the effectiveness of the student's program.

Phyllis G. Wright, Principal
Davison Avenue School
Lynbrook, NY

Student Assistance Program: An Internal Core Team Model

Description

Our school focuses on a prevention-intervention type of "broad-brush" approach when providing help for students with at-risk issues. Today's children often have complex lives and may not be able to cope with confusing events in the world around them. Many experience some form of failure because of their problems.

We feel the school has the responsibility to support each child in reaching his or her greatest potential. We have modeled our program after employee assistance programs designed to address target behaviors that are interfering with student success. Core teams are vital to the success of the program; they employ a mixture of service personnel— teachers, administrators, a school psychologist, and a school nurse. The team offers student support groups as well as one-to-one counseling opportunities, provides class guidance activities, provides good parent communications and education, works with outside referral agencies, and meets monthly to address the needs of the students. The core team also attends a variety of training workshops to upgrade their own skills and abilities.

Benefits

We believe our "Student Assistance Program" (SAP) has assisted students, who otherwise may not have received attention to their specific needs, in becoming healthy, happy individuals. Our referred students exhibit gains in targeted life-skill areas of self-esteem, communication of feelings, interaction skills, and decision making. The SAP core team feels that a child's positive developmental growth is worth any price.

By providing a formalized, systematic approach to identification, referral, intervention, and monitoring, we have the power to affect at-risk students. Students attend school more regularly and know there are resources or support systems available if they need help. This leads to our main goal: students who achieve and, as a result, become lifelong learners equipped with success-oriented personal and social daily-living skills.

Linda Hauser, Principal
Nelson Elementary School
Pinedale, CA

Saturday Scholars

Description

The "Saturday Scholars" are volunteers from the military who tutor, encourage, and spend free time with students. Backed by the chief of naval operations in our community as a "priority" program, the scholars came to our school this year for 6 Saturday mornings from 10:00 a.m. until noon.

Parents were required to sign a permission slip, guarantee transportation, and commit to having their children attend all sessions. The school provided the tutors with a planned curriculum that covered reading, writing, geography, and math skills. On completion of the course, we held a graduation ceremony for the students.

Benefits

"It's a good way to give a part of ourselves back to the community," a volunteer commented. Our tutors reminded us that learning is more than books and papers—it is talking to people and listening to their experiences. It is also a way our children can form partnerships, and even personal relationships, with people in our military community.

Loraine Long Nelson, Principal
Oak Hill Elementary School
Jacksonville, FL

"Turning on" to learning.

Making the Best Use of Technology

Not long ago, "instructional technology" meant films and overhead projectors. Today, computers, CD-ROM, and video offer limitless possibilities for improving the learning process. For example, video allows students to visit the world without leaving their classrooms. Computers allow teachers to meet the unique learning needs of every student.

Finding ways to incorporate this new technology into the curriculum is a challenge. It requires commitment, extensive staff training, and a willingness to experiment.

Many of the Blue Ribbon Schools are leaders in putting today's technology to use. Whether students are producing their own newscasts or are using computers to research topics that interest them, technology has enabled them to "turn on" to learning every day.

"Live" Multimedia

Description

This past year we expanded our multimedia production center. Incorporating the use of computers, CD-ROM, CDs, and audiovisual production equipment, we were able to bring "live" broadcasts into all of our classrooms.

There are numerous ways in which we use the new technology. For example, "live" broadcasts might carry the principal's messages to the whole school, or students can produce events such as geography bees and other contests. We even are able to conduct "live" interviews with special guests before they actually go out and visit the classrooms.

Benefits

Students are receiving valuable experience from working in conjunction with the multimedia center. The "live" broadcasts also help connect people throughout our school.

When guests are visiting, students often greet them announcing, "I know you. I saw you on TV." What a way to make your guest feel welcome on campus!

Solomon W. Kaulukukui, Jr., Principal
Princess Miriam K. Likelike Elementary School
Honolulu, HI

Communicating à la Video

Description

Our school is involved in a project that features the use of television and video production while developing students' communication skills. The premier production, at the moment, is a weekly school news report.

We have set a number of goals for the program. We expect to facilitate students' ability in communicating effectively and in displaying positive attitudes. As they prepare for a video telecast, they acquire and use new planning, production, and editing skills. In addition, the skills of interviewing; listening; and gathering, recording, analyzing, summarizing, and evaluating data are developed. Most important, students have the opportunity to improve higher-level thinking skills, especially their decision-making and problem-solving abilities.

Benefits

The "Video Project" has made a tremendous impact on the development of oral communication skills among our students. Likewise, we have observed that children in the program enjoy increased self-esteem.

We have also experienced a surprise benefit: Our school has noted improved public relations as a result of having the weekly news telecast available for use with parent groups as well as broadcast on local educational television.

Myrna Nishihara, Principal
Daisy Ishihara, Second-Grade Teacher
Mercedes Menor, Gifted and Talented Program
Kapunahala Elementary School
Kaneohe, HI

Electronic Portfolio

Description

For the past 3 years, we have been developing and implementing an "Electronic Portfolio" called the *Grady Profile.* This MacIntosh-based system enables a teacher to readily access pupil, personnel, health, and testing information from classroom workstations.

An important feature of the Grady Profile is its ability to record and store oral reading samples. Later, students and teachers listen together to the work, type in evaluation comments, and save them for use at parent conference time. Writing samples are also taken and are scanned into the computer several times during the year, making possible a variety of comparison and assessment formats.

Benefits

Besides the obvious space-saving advantage, we find that using computers with parents and students has an effect not obtained in other kinds of reporting systems. Everyone seems to be more "tuned in." This use of technology places the teacher in the role of a professional assessing a child's work, pointing out deficiencies and/or positive progress. In this way, emphasis is put on the work rather than on grades, which has been a continuing goal for us.

Our surveys indicate that 97% of both students and their parents feel that our electronic assessment program is superior to the traditional portfolio or the standard report card. We intend to expand this system and look forward to upgraded versions and adaptations of our Electronic Portfolio.

Dr. Kenneth R. Russell, Principal
Bellerive Elementary School
Creve Coeur, MO

Project Interact

Description

We have developed a technology approach called "Project Interact." In this program, teachers bring classes into the Media/Library Center and the Technology Laboratory to fully use all available resources while researching thematic topics.

Students learn to access information through a stacked CD-ROM network center that has an automated card catalog, encyclopedia, and 21 newspapers on line at each terminal. Using cooperative learning groups, the students then assimilate the information they have gathered. Finally, they use a wide variety of technologies—graphics, video digitizing, scanners, and telecommunications—to produce an end product that demonstrates an understanding of new concepts.

Benefits

Our school is fortunate to have an integrated technology program readily available for all students. In Project Interact, learning takes place at multiple levels as students access and assimilate information to complete projects using various technologies. Classes maintain a high interest level while mastering new skills or cooperating with others on assignments.

Linda Klopfenstein, Principal
Dr. Liz Schmitz, Former Principal
Midway Heights Elementary School
Columbia, MO

Computer Pen Pals

Description

Our school has established contact with a central-city campus via a modem connection between schools to facilitate ongoing communications. Last year, students continued "Computer Pen Pal" relationships and shared their own creative compositions on-line.

Next year, we will implement an electronic tutorial program for the inner-city students. Parents of children at our school will be available for students at the central-city school who need extra help. This project is made possible by funding from two grants that we recently received.

Benefits

Communicating by computer has been a valuable adjunct to our curricula. Not only are students more enthusiastic while learning but they also experience the worth of reaching out to others in the community.

We are especially pleased to note that the primary children of both schools have collaborated to produce a hardbound book entitled *Walk Together With Me.*

Sister Margaret Mary Faist, Principal
Lial Elementary School
Whitehouse, OH

Parents as partners in children's education.

 Involving Parents

Parents are a child's first—and most important—teachers. The best schools are successful in part because they have found ways to involve parents in the education of their children; these schools are aware of the relationship between parental involvement and student success.

As Anne T. Henderson noted in *The Evidence Continues to Grow* (1987, Washington, DC: National Committee for Citizens in Education), "Programs designed with strong parent involvement produce students who perform better than otherwise-identical programs that do not involve parents as thoroughly, or that do not involve them at all. Schools that relate well to their communities have student bodies that outperform other schools."

Parent involvement in education can take many forms, as the projects in this chapter illustrate. From efforts to involve parents in making educational decisions to activities parents can do at home to promote learning, the Blue Ribbon Schools are reaching out to make parents true partners in their children's education.

The Goal Team

Description

Our school has a "Program Team" made up of parents, teachers, and students. This team determines the goals for the upcoming year and evaluates the outcome of objectives from the previous year. Another responsibility of the team is to provide a needs assessment of the school.

The team eventually meets with the board of education to have its goals approved. Team representatives then share the results and any concerns with the public.

Benefits

By cooperating with their children and the staff, parents are taking responsibility for improving our school. Activities such as open house, school-grade and team-level coffees, newsletters, school volunteering, the arts alive program, and international day bring hundreds of parents into the school to assist with the education of our students. Involved parents mean supportive parents, and that makes all the difference!

Benjamin Davenport, Principal
Eastern Middle School
Riverside, CT

Guest Readers

Description

We want children at our school to learn to read and *love* to read. We have found that "Guest Readers"—administrators, parents, business partners, district personnel, senior citizens, or even other students—help us accomplish this objective.

Each day students listen to quality literature of high interest. Guests often bring their own books, or one is provided. We also make sure that children are able to spend time reading books during their language arts instruction periods.

Benefits

Everyone benefits. Students hear a worthwhile story and see that reading is something for everyone. The staff members include our guests in the teaching and learning process, which encourages better home-school-community relations. Best of all, the children are enjoying books.

Dee Knabb, Principal
Nob Hill Elementary School
Sunrise, FL

PALs

Description

Parents are "PALs" at our school. The parent-assisted learning (PAL) program was initiated several years ago by the kindergarten and first-grade teachers as a way to involve every parent.

PAL packets are sent home with students several times during the week on a rotating basis. The packets contain games and activities that are designed for parents to complete with their children, along with a book to read to them.

At a special year-end ceremony, parents who have worked with their children on a regular basis receive a blue and gold PAL pin along with a certificate.

Benefits

The program has been such a success that now all grades join in. Activities encourage parents to listen to their children read, to help them master math facts, and to participate together on special projects. The PAL packets are one component of the school PAL program, which includes a parent volunteer program, a parent/teacher organization, and parent education workshops.

Beth Kellerhals, Principal
Graysville Elementary School
Graysville, GA

Science Discovery Room

Description

If your parent organization is a bit weary of the usual activities, such as fund-raising, chaperoning, tutoring, and the like, then empower your parents as partners in learning by inviting them to commit to the development of a supplementary learning center.

At our school, parents established such a center several years ago. The entire community has become involved and still contributes resources to extend and to develop more hands-on science activities for our children.

Benefits

The "Science Discovery Room" provides a way for many people to be a part of our school. It continues to be a source of pride for parents, teachers, students, and our neighborhood.

Shirley C. Hayashi, Principal
Mililani-uka Elementary School
Mililani, HI

Hooray for All Parents

Description

We have 100% participation at our fall parent and teacher conferences. It is a tradition, and we work hard to make it happen.

Our parents and staff believe it is essential that this event be well-attended. If parents do not have transportation to the school, the principals provide rides. Even if our extended evening hours (until 7:00 p.m.) are inconvenient, we go to the homes of the children or to their parents' place of employment to conduct this high-priority conference.

Benefits

Because students respond so positively to this visible support from parents and teachers, we are all willing to give extra time, if necessary, to attain full participation in the parent conference idea. We all believe it is worth the effort.

Ardis Wipf, Principal
Klondike Elementary School
West Lafayette, IN

Friday Knight Club

Description

The "Friday Knight Club," an alternative to drugs, was implemented at our school by an active parent group. This weekly event came about in order for students to have a safe, drug-free Friday night option, and somewhere to be other than the mall.

Benefits

Up to one-third of our student body attends the Friday Knight Club. Music, sports, board games, pizza-sharing, and other activities offer these young people opportunities to make friends and to socialize in a positive environment. The evening is both sponsored and chaperoned by parents and is monetarily totally self-supporting.

Do you know where your children are on Friday nights? WE DO!

Robert L. Wilson, Principal
Oxford Middle School
Overland Park, KS

Parents Go to School

Description

Parent involvement in schools means more than participating in volunteer groups or having conferences with teachers. It also has to do with educating parents to understand what we teach, how we teach, and why we teach in a certain way.

Each year, we offer parent-education sessions in which we focus on one or two curriculum areas. By limiting the number of topics we discuss, we feel we can give our parents an in-depth understanding of each subject.

To accommodate the lives and schedules of our parents, we have been flexible in how the educational seminars are organized. For example, parents may choose whether they would like to attend a morning, noon, or evening session.

Benefits

As a result of these meetings, parents now have a greater understanding of what we do. We are pleased to find that fewer parents question why their children are not being taught exactly as they were.

Adrienne Jones Crockett, Principal
Eastover Elementary School
Bloomfield Hills, MI

Spice of Life

Description

Frequently, you will find a special section entitled "The ›Spice of Life" in grade-level newsletters at our school. For those who want to pep up their lives, this column offers a little extra spice to learning in the form of enrichment projects.

The newsletter suggestions can be done either at school, after assigned work has been completed, or at home. The choice to add spice to one's life is totally voluntary. "Spices" vary by subject so that interested students can sample a variety of tasty experiences.

Benefits

Many students have collaborated with their parents to accomplish amazing projects. By the way, SPICE is an acronym for Studious Pupils Indeed Cherish Education!

Joanne Y. Olson, Principal
Mounds Park Academy - Lower School
St. Paul, MN

Friday Folder

Description

We have developed a simple, yet effective, method of communicating with the parents of our children. The scope of the entire parent program is multifaceted; however, our best idea is the "Friday Folder."

We send home a folder with each student every Friday. It contains a weekly calendar from the principal that lists all events at the school. The principal also includes a weekly "tip sheet." On it are suggestions to help parents make the home learning process easier.

Friday Folders are also filled with all the graded papers and assignments completed by the student during the week.

In this way, parents are provided with regular updates of what is happening in the classroom. The folders are returned to the teachers each Monday morning, signed by the parents to indicate they have reviewed the contents.

Benefits

Our parent involvement program was selected as the best in our state. The folder is one example of how our parents cooperate with us while, at the same time, becoming better informed. Because they are aware that all material is sent home on Fridays, the project goes smoothly and communication is effective.

Dr. Ernest Palestis, Principal/Superintendent
Canfield Avenue School
Mine Hill, NJ

Weekly Principal's Breakfast

Description

We have discovered a wonderful way to bring parents and the community into our school. A weekly breakfast, from 7:30 a.m. to 9:00 a.m. each Tuesday, allows easy and consistent access to the principal.

At the meetings, there is no agenda. Everyone is invited. The group size ranges from 1 to 25 people. The principal and the guests share ideas, express concerns, and discuss philosophy together. The Parent-Teacher Association provides the refreshments and the principal provides the coffee.

Benefits

We are pleased with the informal nature of the "Weekly Principal's Breakfast." We find that it is a nonthreatening and positive way to maintain a connection with those who have an interest in us but who are outside the day-to-day life on campus.

Dr. Mary Lou Clayton, Principal
Robert E. Lee Elementary School
Austin, TX

Family Enrichment Center

Description

Our school is opening the door of opportunity for parents and community members to continue their education at the Chapter 1 "Family Enrichment Center." Courses are offered in a variety of subjects and with differing degrees of difficulty.

If parents want to improve their skills, they may choose, for example, the best level of instruction for them in the areas of reading, language, or math. There are all types of courses available, including life/survival skills, computer literacy, English as a Second Language, and Graduate Equivalency Diploma (GED) preparation.

The Enrichment Center is located in the computer-assisted instruction lab at our school. A teacher and a paraprofessional trained to work with parents are on duty on Saturday mornings to provide extra assistance and encouragement.

In addition, we hold sessions on the art of parenting. We provide information about how to help with homework, how television affects children, and how to set realistic goals. The center also makes it possible to prepare parents for getting the most out of conferences with teachers.

Benefits

This program is an all-around success. Whether for self-improvement or to better understand and help their children in the learning experience, our parents are attending the Family Enrichment Center.

Faye Webb, Principal
Mirabeau B. Lamar Elementary School
Corpus Christi, TX

Students on Saturday

Description

Project "Students on Saturday" (SOS) is the ultimate program to involve parents at our school. Parents become the experts in teaching curricula to students and also have an opportunity to spend more time with their children.

We offer two 45-minute classes for students. Sessions can be held on any Saturdays when there are parents who wish to participate. Parents and the principal plan the entire program; they also solicit other parents and community members to do the teaching.

The parents target each offering to specific grade levels. We have been fortunate to have such interesting sessions as astronomy, baseball, cheerleading, ceramics, money, blacksmithing, photography, and kung fu. We have learned about our mountain heritage and discovered other countries. Our parents help highlight the different seasons and make us more aware of ourselves and the great outdoors.

Benefits

The SOS elective event gives our children an opportunity to spend Saturday mornings in a constructive manner. We have had over 200 students register. Students, parents, and the principal all show up to learn together.

The SOS program offers an educational opportunity beyond that available in regular classrooms or during the school day. It also helps us use the expertise at hand from members of the community.

Dr. Barbara J. Fassig, Principal
Elm Grove Elementary School
Wheeling, WV

Teachers as important professionals.

Encouraging Teacher Professionalism

If children are our nation's most important resource, then teachers have the most important job in our society.

Today, the best schools have found ways to treat teachers like the professionals they are. In these schools, teachers share ideas about what works—and what does not. They demonstrate their expertise for their colleagues, they brainstorm about ways to enhance learning opportunities for all children, and they are as actively involved in learning and growth as their students.

The Blue Ribbon School projects included in this chapter offer illustrations of how schools are enhancing teacher professionalism. They have found ways to give teachers time to plan cooperatively, they empower teachers to make decisions that affect them, and they take teachers out of the isolation of their classrooms and encourage them to share with colleagues.

Literature Linkup

Description

To use "Literature Linkup" with students, teachers arrange a time with the librarian to show videotapes of literary selections in the library. These tapes are available from our district media library, and each school has a set of tapes. Selections cover 1 hour of literature.

An outstanding pupil or a teacher aide views the selections in advance and prepares comprehension and appreciation questions. These are read to the children before the viewing and are discussed in depth afterwards.

While the class watches and discusses the selections, the teachers meet in another room and work on their own projects, plans, or paperwork. At the end of the hour, they meet their classes in the library. Teachers may use this service up to twice a month by making arrangements with the librarian.

Benefits

Literature Linkup provides extra planning time for teachers during the students' day. At the same time, our children have an opportunity to appreciate and understand literature typically not found in a basal reading series.

Dr. Beverly DeMott, Principal
N. B. Broward Elementary School
Tampa, FL

Teacher Triads

Description

"Teacher Triads" are an integral part of our professional development program. An offshoot of cooperative-learning triads, they encourage three staff members to work together to share ideas, to plan lessons, to team teach, and to process results.

Each team consists of a previously trained "expert" in the area of cooperative learning. A second member has limited knowledge of triads from taking workshops and through reading, and the third person is a novice.

In some instances, one member might substitute for another's class so that the person can observe a cooperative-learning lesson being led by the expert. At other times, the expert teacher's class is taught by one of the team, and the expert models or peer coaches new skills to the third team member.

The cooperative-learning triads expanded to professional triads, spreading to all areas of the curriculum and to other teaching strategies; that is, novel studies, hands-on science and math, and so forth. Teachers are encouraged to work with each other and to support their colleagues.

Benefits

We are successfully using the Teacher Triads system for creating collegiality, sharing craft knowledge, promoting professionalism, and using time efficiently in an already overworked system. The professional teams have had a positive effect on the entire staff and student body. Cooperation and collaboration have become an integral part of what we teach and do at our school.

Edward A. Tatro
Arnold J. Tyler School
New Lenox, IL

Musical Teamwork

Description

The most unique characteristic about our school is the way we combine cooperative teaming with music. Several years ago, we formed a staff singing group to develop friendships and to have fun.

Our secondary purpose in singing is to provide good public relations with the community as we perform for various civic groups throughout the year. Our music group is voluntary, and we rehearse two mornings a month.

Benefits

We include both talented and less talented, albeit enthusiastic, singers in our group. We present a good example of
team spirit, sharing our love of learning and our commitment to children with the public.

Patty Gritzfeld, Principal
Longfellow Elementary School
Scottsbluff, NE

Time to Reflect

Description

We sponsor an annual middle-level learners' conference
in collaboration with a nearby sister school. All of our teachers are encouraged to prepare a presentation on some aspect
of education. We distribute an invitation and a brochure,
complete with titles and descriptions of the talks, to state
district schools. Typically, hundreds of educators from the
area attend.

Benefits

Sponsoring this conference accomplishes many things. It
provides an ongoing in-service experience for our staff. It
also allows teachers a time of "reflected supervision" as they
write their presentations. For those who participate, the
conference encourages self-actualization, which in turn promotes enthusiasm toward new roles and responsibilities.

Dr. Robert L. Furman, Principal
Boyce Middle School
Upper St. Clair, PA

Site-Based Decision Making

Description

Through "Site-Based Decision-Making," our teachers have been given a new role of shared leadership in the classroom. They have become more actively involved in decisions that affect them day to day.

Examples of situations in which teachers have been responsible for a content-area action are: (a) overriding the requirement to give numerical grades in social studies and science, and choosing pass or fail marks instead; and (b) overriding the requirement of handwriting workbooks for fifth and sixth graders.

Benefits

Both of the above teacher suggestions ultimately have affected performance outcomes of students through tailored teaching designs. The idea of teacher ownership has benefited our school and has developed feelings of trust and open communication among all members of our school staff.

Dr. Carol M. Hutson, Principal
Glendale Middle School
Nashville, TN

Individualized Goals

Description

A major project at our school has been the implementation of a portfolio assessment system that encourages innovation among teachers who want to individualize their professional goals.

At the beginning of the year, teacher participants jointly plan with the principal an area of professional growth, and together they develop specific personal objectives. Midyear and summary conferences provide ongoing follow-up as the projects are activated.

In staff meetings, teachers present their portfolios to colleagues. This year's projects included a prekindergarten program that called for parental involvement, the compilation of a process-writing student portfolio, an integrated disciplined-based art education program, a fifth-grade/kindergarten "buddy" system, the teaching of reading through music and choral readings, and a buildingwide mentor writing instructor.

Benefits

We find that the portfolio assessment system helps teachers reach their professional goals, provides appropriate resources and support, and rewards well-thought-out risk taking. Staff members, in return, feel recognized and appreciated as exemplary professional leaders.

Janie Milner, Principal
Saigling Elementary School
Plano, TX

Staff Lock-In

Description

At the beginning of the year, we hold a "Staff Lock-In" that lasts 6 hours and includes dinner and snacks. We have the opportunity to get to know each other better and to renew our commitment to the school.

We divide into teams and participate in activities that increase our expertise in team building. Each of us is asked to help create a school vision, which results in a clearer understanding of our school's goals.

Benefits

Our staff unites in its intention to ensure that all students have a successful learning experience. This attitude is particularly vital, because we have a high at-risk student population. As a result, we have experienced a strong team spirit and an atmosphere of trust throughout the year.

Sue Romanowsky, Principal
Francone Elementary School
Houston, TX

Knowing What to Expect

Description

Our principal lets staff and incoming teachers know exactly what is expected of them before they begin classes. We receive a list of helpful instructions about our duties.

There are five major areas of importance for us to master. We are encouraged to be enthusiastic and innovative, to develop proficient classroom management skills, to work effectively with parents, to cooperate with staff members, and to undergo technology training.

We are challenged from the beginning to give of our best. When we examine the fine print on our instruction list, we may find some tasks that require new skills or call for an extra amount of energy to complete.

For example, we are expected to (a) work willingly with a team beyond school hours (3:30 p.m.) on a regular basis, (b) never display a negative or moody attitude, (c) never gossip, (d) invite parents into the classroom to participate, (e) operate a computer lab and integrate multimedia into the curriculum, and (f) write grants to provide enrichment opportunities for students.

Benefits

By informing teachers of what is expected, our principal enlists the support of the staff, models excellence, and prevents unhappy surprises.

Claudia Tousek, Principal
Highland Park Elementary School
Austin, TX

Committees All Around

Description

Every staff member, including aides and custodians, serves on a committee at our school. Staff members volunteer for the committee on which they wish to serve each fall. Care is taken to ensure that there is broad representation on each committee.

There are several committees with explicitly stated missions in the school. A staff development committee is responsible for professional growth issues; a home-school relations committee plans parent involvement activities; and a health, safety, and wellness committee suggests alternative meals and snacks in the cafeteria and promotes events in the school that highlight wellness. There is a committee to organize schoolwide events, a committee to address schoolwide discipline issues, and a school improvement team to identify school goals.

Our committees have budgets that are used to support their missions. Team leaders, who are on the school improvement team, cochair the committees so that all our efforts are coordinated with the school goals.

Benefits

The committee structure involves teachers in active decision making and contributes to teacher empowerment. Because they have considerable input, staff members have had a significant and positive influence on what happens at our school.

John D. Briggs, Principal
Dr. Carol S. Beers, Former Principal
Rawls Byrd Elementary School
Williamsburg, VA

Senior citizens as partners.

Building Community-School/ Business-School Partnerships

Strong schools make strong communities. The quality of the local school system is a critical factor when companies are making a decision to relocate. Without an educated workforce, American business cannot hope to compete in the global marketplace.

Because schools, communities, and businesses are so interdependent, they often find ways to work together. Whether it is providing support for innovative projects, acting as mentors, or volunteering, businesses and communities have a vital role to play in today's schools.

Blue Ribbon Schools reach out to their communities, and they have created partnerships that enable the schools to do a better job of meeting the needs of all children. The projects in this chapter include partnerships with businesses, senior citizens, law enforcement officers, and college students. These collaborations help schools provide individual attention to students, enrich learning opportunities, and encourage innovation.

Schools, too, are reaching out to their communities. In some of the projects described in this chapter, schools are offering needed assistance to their communities.

Seed Money

Description

Several years ago, representatives from three school districts in our county joined forces with interested businesses to form the nonprofit Public Schools Foundation of Tippecanoe County, Inc., a corporation that solicits donations from both individuals and businesses. The "Seed Money" invested by the foundation soon built up to a substantial amount through the support of the community; the Seed Money for grants grows and is available annually for class projects.

Each year, teachers write grant proposals for projects they would like to do. A reception is held every April to announce the winners of the funding. Dozens of ideas and innovative activities have received amounts of up to $1,500.

The money cannot be used to pay teachers, but it can be designated to hire artists, to buy materials, or to pay for workshops. Past projects have included an evening of family writing, a collection of celebrities pledging allegiance on tape, materials for a first-grade take-home reading kit, and the creation of a classroom pet-lending "library" complete with caged pets.

Benefits

Our Seed Money has made possible numerous projects that would never have happened otherwise. The grant proposal form is easy to complete and has encouraged teachers to refine their creative ideas. And, most important, the foundation system rewards teachers with money to implement their ideas.

Ardis Wipf, Principal
Lorie Sparks, Assistant Principal
Klondike Elementary School
West Lafayette, IN

Brown-Bag Buddies

Description

The "Brown-Bag Buddies" program promotes community- and business-school partnerships. We invite individuals from local companies to have lunch with some of our students one day a week.

At the beginning of the year, businesses are requested to participate, and students also are asked to indicate their interest. The school counselor then matches the sponsors with students who want a buddy.

Benefits

Both students and business representatives report that they love sharing this time. They look forward to getting to know their buddy at lunch each week, and many request to repeat the program the following year.

Jane McAuliffe, Principal
Sheila Harrison-Bentley, Counselor
Kaye Berman, Third-Grade Teacher
William Daniel Alexander, Former Principal
Candlewood Elementary School
Rockville, MD

Grand Friendships

Description

Our township has a large number of retirement communities that have proven to be a vital resource for two programs at our school.

In the "Grandfriends" program, each class is "adopted" by a senior citizen who does grandparent-type things for them once or twice a month. Activities "grandfriends" share with students include reading to the class, speaking about a career or hobby, showing pictures and telling about their travel, baking cookies, and helping with class projects.

In return, students send birthday and holiday cards to their "grandfriends" and invite them to all school events such as the Interest Fair, school concerts, and the school picnic.

In the "Senior Pen Pal" program, students in Grades 1 through 3 correspond with senior citizens on a regular basis. Many seniors send postcards from their trips. At the end of the year, a "pen pal encounter" is planned and the elders come to school to meet their student friends.

Benefits

Fostering positive relationships with senior residents is important for the community and for the school. Our senior projects are a wonderful way to promote intergenerational awareness. An additional big plus is that many of the activities lend themselves to developing writing skills.

Nancy G. Richmond, Principal
Mill Lake School
Spotswood, NJ

Reading Clinic

Description

Our school has developed a partnership with two higher education institutions in the area. The "Reading Clinic" at a nearby university has begun to place clinicians in our school as part of their internship. A relationship with another university permits certain college courses in education to be held on our campus.

Benefits

We feel that the interchanges we are making with professionals at the nearby universities provide an exceptional opportunity to enrich the learning of our students. Not only do the elementary school students receive quality instruction but the college students also can be with the children on a frequent basis, affording a good understanding of what it is like to be a classroom teacher.

Dr. Andrea Roth Stein, Principal
Como Park Elementary School
Lancaster, NY

Bears That Care

Description

We supply teddy bears to local law enforcement officers for children in extremely stressful situations. The bears help to calm youngsters involved in accidents, fires, or difficult domestic situations. Officers carry bears in their cruisers as essential equipment.

Benefits

The Norman D. Bear project was initiated by first graders, and now service organizations, along with middle and high school student groups, contribute enough funding to supply hundreds of bears. Student Council members supervise tagging and bagging the bears. The project represents our caring school and sets a positive image in the community.

Gloria R. Clouse, Principal
Normandy Elementary School
Centerville, OH

Reading for Paw Prints

Description

Our business partnership has focused on meaningful student academic achievement. One component of the agenda has been an independent reading program.

This year, teachers set a predetermined independent reading goal for each student. To keep everyone focused, monthly award certificates marked students' accomplishments. In the Adopt-a-School partnership building, we displayed "bear paws" identifying the children and the number of books each had read.

By the end of the year, "bear prints" were everywhere, and our program was firmly established.

Benefits

In this school-business alliance, teachers and partners successfully encourage students to reach learning goals appropriate to their abilities. Motivated students are continually recognized, and everyone reaching the reading goal receives a bear-paw pin.

Carolyn C. Wood, Principal
Brookmeade Elementary School
Nashville, TN

Bank Day

Description

Community-school-business partnerships are growing at our school. We have ongoing programs with several large corporations, Junior Achievement, and a local bank.

Our bank partner has set up a School Savings Program with its consumer banking division. A four-way collaboration among the bank, school districts, parents, and students is designed to teach children the fundamentals of finance, practical money management, and financial responsibility.

Teachers integrate the 3-week bank curriculum into their lessons. Each week on "Bank Day," students use school computers and software provided by the bank to make deposits to their personal savings accounts.

Benefits

Our bank partnership makes it possible for students to gain a practical understanding of saving and handling money. Even the parents are involved: Volunteers provide a vital program link by serving as tellers in the school bank.

Jane Farney, Principal
Lowery Elementary School
Houston, TX

Hands-On Partners

Description

A grant from a corporate business partner funded equipment and supplies for a hands-on science enrichment program at our school. In the lab, trained volunteers facilitate fourth and fifth graders in both the physical and life sciences. Study units include lessons about atomic structure, earth changes, energy, and animal physiology.

Another successful partnership promoted a family math program that encourages children and parents to explore concepts collaboratively. Through hands-on experiences, parents learn about the latest problem-solving strategies nationally recommended for the math curriculum.

A special program called STARS—Students Through Arts Reaching Success—integrates arts education into the classroom. Six performances by our city opera were incorporated into thematic units in music, language, and theater arts.

Benefits

A Campus Advisory Team assists in implementing site-based decisions, such as the development of the hands-on math and science projects. Not only are parents included but we also actively pursue the support of both community and business partnerships. We are fortunate to have these valuable enrichment programs as a consequence of community cooperation with our school.

James K. Felle, Principal
Nottingham Elementary School
Houston, TX

Night School

Description

For the past 6 years, our school staff and the Parent-Teacher Association (PTA) have hosted a Friday "Night School" for the third, fourth, and fifth grades. Each Night School has a special topic or focus; we have targeted mathematics, science, visual and performing arts, and technology.

Phase 1 of the evening allows students to rotate among presenters who share how the evening's topic is used in business crafts. Phase 2 offers hands-on activities, also related to the topic of the evening.

From about 1:30 a.m. until 6:30 a.m., the children are encouraged to rest or sleep on bedrolls they have brought along. They eat a light breakfast we serve at 7:00 a.m. on Saturday morning, and then they go home with their parents.

Benefits

This annual event is extremely popular and has become a well-known tradition for our young people. It is a learning endeavor that creates a unique, exciting experience, encourages parent and community-business involvement, and helps students realize the broader applications of school-based learning. Many people in our community cooperate to make Night School a success.

Dr. Marla W. McGhee, Principal
Live Oak Elementary School
Austin, TX

Economics Everywhere

Description

We participate in an economics educational concept in conjunction with a nearby university and the State Council for Economics Education. Our school is one of the first in our state to offer such a program for kindergarten through eighth-grade students.

When we began 5 years ago, each teacher met with a university economics professor to set up objectives and skills appropriate to the developmental abilities of differing levels. To prevent having another subject to teach, they integrated the economics lessons into the regular curriculum.

Students and teachers have access to an extensive resource library of books, videos, games, and computer programs at the university. A graduate student liaison meets monthly with teachers to discuss progress, to make any necessary adjustments in the curriculum, and to coordinate the program with university faculty.

Students learn about economic interactions and interrelationships with family, community, state, nation, and the world. Field trips and speakers involving local retailers, banks, utilities, stockbrokers, and government law enforcement agencies demonstrate how economics affects the quality of our lives.

Benefits

Our economics program partners introduce students to this subject not as abstract theory but as a process and a skill for making wise consumer decisions that affect everyday living. Throughout all the grades, children discover how they are influenced by economics. The Junior Achievement Center assists teachers with business basics for sixth- and eighth-grade classes. As part of the state history curriculum, fourth graders sponsor a Native American barter fair to experience the development of trade and money. Fifth and sixth grades set up a business that provides either a product or a service. At the end of the year, they organize an economics fair for the entire student body to practice comparative shopping and other wise consumer skills. The eighth grade, with the guidance of a local stockbroker, competes in a stock investment project sponsored by *USA TODAY.* This year, one of our teams won first place against middle and high schools in our region.

Sister Carmella Campione, Principal
Our Lady of Fatima School
Huntington, WV

Cooperating Community

Description

Our school is a member of a consortium of local not-for-profit agencies, government groups, educators, businesses, churches, social service agencies, and area residents that provides support for a low-income housing complex in our attendance area.

We meet at least monthly to identify areas of potential concern, to plan prevention and intervention strategies, to share resources, and to celebrate achievements.

Benefits

From our partnership a number of collaborative grants have emerged that have made innovative school programs possible, including full-day kindergarten and stipends for parents who assist at school. Participating in this venture assures us of access to needed resources and ongoing community support for educational endeavors. If concerns or questions arise, we know exactly whom to contact to develop a proactive response.

Dr. David M. Bray, Principal
Kathryn Price, Home-School Coordinator
John Muir Elementary School
Madison, WI

The joy of learning.

Restructuring Efforts and School Improvement

B lue Ribbon Schools believe, "If we always do what we've always done, we'll always get what we always got." These schools are characterized by a commitment to continuous improvement and a willingness to try new approaches.

The innovative programs described in this chapter illustrate some of the ways in which American schools are changing. They expect students to think critically and solve problems—and they have found ways to help them meet those goals: They are developing new ways to organize classrooms based on children's needs, not just on their ages; they are empowering students and teachers to make decisions; and they are striving to become places where students and staff members are nurtured and encouraged to grow.

There is no single way to reform schools, but in the exciting programs in this chapter, it is possible to get a glimpse of what all schools should look like in the 21st century.

Strategy Room

Description

The Strategy/Multiple Intelligences Program was designed to support preparation of our children for the 21st century.

This classroom, influenced by Dr. Howard Gardner's theory that the seven areas of intelligence overlap, provides children with inter- and intrapersonal time as they interact with carefully selected games, participate in a musical or spatial activity, or learn together in the areas of humanities, math, science, and social studies. Students explore individual interests and abilities not necessarily tapped by the typical school curriculum. The opportunity offered by the "Strategy Room" for exploration and self-choice is designed to enhance morale and to build confidence. By working through some of the problems involved in the activities offered, the students acquire self-confidence in their problem-solving skills, abilities to follow rules, integration of thought and action, imagination, social skills, and self-motivation.

The Strategy Room has become an interactive think tank. The guided activities promote a sharing and caring attitude as students develop attitudes that reflect an understanding and acceptance of others. Humanity, human rights, and human relations share top billing with all subject matter and activities.

Benefits

Each student's activity selections and interactions are documented, providing an intellectual profile from which a better understanding of the student's strengths, interests, and learning style can be drawn. The purpose is to spark the energy and the creativity that exist in each child by bringing a new challenge to the educational environment, recognizing that the possibilities are endless.

Charlene D. Bush, Principal
Janice Gritton, Strategies Teacher
Virginia Wheeler Elementary School
Louisville, KY

Extension Program

Description

The "Extension Program" prepares pupils who need intensive professional support for a less restrictive learning environment than the traditional stand-alone, self-contained special education classroom. Our teachers have a firm commitment to teams and to individualized programming as the way to help special students get ready for the mainstream.

In the mornings, the children may leave their assigned homerooms to spend an uninterrupted 45 minutes of reading instruction in small same-level groupings. Next, they participate in larger groups working on fine or large motor development, art, music, or computer-related activities. Some groups have up to 16 pupils, assisted by two or three paraprofessionals and/or specialists. The children may be helped by as many as seven teachers each day.

Benefits

The sustained reading period has resulted in dramatic gains in achievement. Entering pupils are accommodated easily into the groupings at appropriate levels, and students can be moved to other groups as they advance. The Extension Program lets pupils practice needed social and independence skills when, for example, they are walking independently to class between periods. They learn to relate to several adults and many different students in the process of changing classes during the day. Larger group activities teach skills that are useful for success in regular classrooms, such as patience in taking turns, working independently, and managing time and materials.

Perhaps the greatest benefit of the program for teachers has been the esprit de corps engendered by planning cooperatively with staff and working consistently with the same students. At team meetings, we enjoy pulling together to handle difficult behavior or sharing ideas and materials for specific students. Paraprofessionals also feel that their talents are fully used because they often plan and lead group activities.

For the third year in a row, staff members have voted a resounding "yes!" to continue this approach to programming for our special students.

Dr. Sherry L. Liebes, Principal
Frances R. Fuchs, Special Center
Beltsville, MD

Primary Roundup

Description

Our school has restructured Grades 1 and 2 to create a multi-age primary unit. A teacher has his or her students for 2 years, with half of the class entering the primary classroom each year. Before school begins, teachers establish partnerships with parents by visiting with them and their child at home. The team of teachers develops the curriculum around themes and embraces a whole-language approach to teaching.

Our best idea is "Primary Roundup," held every morning in the foyer for 30 minutes. Children's voices are heard throughout the halls as all four primary classrooms gather to sing, to chant, and to learn together. On a weekly rotating basis, one teacher leads, one plays the piano or operates the tape recorder, and the others participate with students, using music as a tool to develop emergent readers. Large charts display songs that are sung over and over, becoming part of "I Can Read" folders. Students often use motions or dramatize songs relating to themes of study.

As the children progress through the year, they share some of their learning with other classes. We have had as many as 40 visitors as the word went out about Primary Roundup. We also conducted a session in the gym where over 60 parents participated with their children.

Benefits

Roundup provides a powerful learning opportunity and also serves as a marvelous public relations tool. Those who drop by our school get to view this exciting educational format right in the foyer. Visiting parents now better understand whole-language learning. In addition, teachers have increased their skills and have become a stronger team, supporting and appreciating each other's gifts. Ultimately, our students gain a unity-building experience; no one can sit through Primary Roundup and have a bad day!

Dr. Beth S. Randklev, Principal
Belmont Elementary School
Grand Forks, ND

Nitty-Gritty Committee

Description

Because our staff has more than doubled in 1 year, we decided to bring teachers into the decision-making process while providing for efficient communication.

Grade-level representatives on the advisory committee take charge of the "nitty-gritties" that often foul up the mechanism of a school. They take responsibility for scheduling, fire drill procedures, recess protocol and problems, and the like. Teachers have only to drop a note about a concern or a suggestion in the chairperson's mailbox, and a brief meeting is scheduled to address the matter. Each committee member then communicates any decisions to grade-level team members for a final approval.

A second schoolwide committee has been charged with determining subjects for in-service days. This Professional Development Committee uses a consensus-building model to determine topics that teachers want to investigate.

Benefits

Our school runs much more smoothly and pleasantly with active teacher participation. For example, in-service days have become days of professional growth that teachers anticipate.

Rita M. Klein, Principal
Dorothea H. Simmons School
Horsham, PA

Sharing the RICE Process

Description

Personal excellence in a warm, friendly environment is a tradition at our private, coeducational preschool-8 elementary school. To grow along with our diverse student body, we have established an institutional program to restructure the entire school community.

We seek to accomplish four major shifts. In setting new goals, we facilitate staff action in movement from (a) central authority to shared *Responsibility*, (b) a hierarchical worldview to global *Interdependence*, (c) viewing knowledge as static to dynamic *Creativity*, and (d) a local viewpoint to people *Empowerment*—RICE.

After 3 years of intensive planning involving administration, faculty, parents, students, and the curriculum administration, our school has received approval to use the RICE process as a priority educational tool. We are establishing a practical model by outlining a comprehensive worldview, a consistent ethic of life, a peacemaking model, and skills for the global village. Our strategies encompass four umbrella areas: visioning, staff development, curriculum development, and networking programs.

Benefits

The RICE process has challenged us to a sustained, focused, and multiyear effort. We have improved in articulating and focusing ideas, involving the community more critically through evaluation opportunities, using funding effectively, and planning our future more intentionally. We already have seen gains in our school structure, and we plan to publish a manual using the RICE process to assist other schools in their restructuring endeavors.

Sister Elizabeth McCoy, acj, Director
Ancillae-Assumpta Academy
Wyncote, PA

Satisfied Staff

Description

To nurture and empower our staff, we provide numerous professional development opportunities.

All staff members begin the year by discovering more about their working styles with a Myers-Briggs assessment. Next, classroom teams sign up to host one of our monthly socials—events ranging from secret pals and favorite-vacation pictures, to poem-writing contests. They always bring plenty of food, too!

We have Wednesday meetings, alternating between grade-level and all-faculty sessions. The entire staff discusses school philosophy, discipline, and activities common to all youngsters, from ages 3 to 14. Grade-level teachers talk about the curriculum, cooperative learning, and ideas that work.

The school pays for half the cost of workshops, and, in return, participants inform the rest of us. Often, a teacher offers a miniseminar in a specific area such as drawing, nutrition, or the use of computers. We collaborate on all-school events—food drives, parent night, or student council projects—first talking out details and later recapping during postprogram sessions to decide how we might make changes or improvements.

Occasionally, we open meetings with compliments to each other, and we take time to list personal celebrations of our staff in a weekly news memo.

Benefits

Involving faculty in decisions that affect students engenders heightened interest and commitment. At our independent school, we feel it is well worth the effort to gather teacher input and establish teams. We hope everyone is celebrated both by being listened to and by being included.

For example, before teachers leave for summer vacation, they help set the next year's calendar, give input into class placement, and list necessary materials. Local high school students are hired to help pack up and close the building, and teachers spend a full day taking stock of what worked. By inviting next year's incoming faculty to our year-end party, we can welcome our coworkers to a place where staff development is important.

Dr. Patricia Feltin, Principal
Eton School
Bellevue, WA

Community of Learners

Description

Our principal wrote a letter to parents, staff, and students acknowledging the contributions of the "Community of Learners" in carrying forth our mission. We intend to empower each child with attitudes, knowledge, and skills for lifelong learning. It takes all of us working together to provide an environment that values curiosity, challenge, cooperation, creative and critical thinking, and respect.

The volunteer efforts, open communication, and high interest and expectations of parents motivate everyone, staff and children alike. Staff members continually share their knowledge and enthusiasm for learning with colleagues and are models for children.

In addition, our curriculum promotes student independence and inquiry, emphasizing research, writing, and problem solving. Instead of using textbooks and workbooks, pupils read quality literature using original documents. Most important, children are given many opportunities to work cooperatively, not competitively.

Benefits

Students learn from students, teachers learn from parents, parents learn from teachers, teachers learn from teachers, children learn from parents, teachers learn from students, and students learn from teachers. The joy, quality, and modeling of learning at our school are exemplary.

Harlan G. Siebrecht, Principal
Crestwood Elementary School
Madison, WI

P.S. That's the principal!

Even More "Best Ideas!"

The best schools have much in common—but they are also unique. This chapter includes some innovative programs that do not fit neatly into any of the preceding chapters.

The programs included in this chapter are as individual as the schools that developed them, yet they all reflect the Blue Ribbon Schools' emphasis on meeting children's needs. From a new way to assess student performance to an effort to build positive relationships with students, the programs developed by these schools focus on meeting children's needs.

Reading and Writing Assessment

Description

At our school, the assessment process for reading and writing is designed to gather information about how students use their literacy skills on a day-to-day basis in the relaxed settings of the classroom, the library, the playground, and the home. In addition, this process considers information about how students compare to state and national standards.

Teacher observations and professional judgment comments are recorded on student outcome cards. In the classroom, teachers observe students in a variety of settings and are best qualified to provide an ongoing "video" of each child's activities.

A standardized test, by contrast, delivers only a one-time "snapshot" of a student. As a result, tests are included as a part of a teacher's database, but testing is not the most significant method of assessing student progress.

Benefits

Our performance assessment program in reading and writing recognizes the wealth of communication knowledge and experience students bring with them to school. Teachers support experimentation with language in their classes and highlight the best materials available. They also model and incorporate the effective use of reading and writing as tools for lifelong learning.

The program includes staff development sessions to assist teachers in refining their observational strategies. This process is an adjunct to testing that validates teachers' judgments, enhances professional skills, and encourages collegial dialogues about the learning process.

Dr. Karen L. List, Principal
Eric G. Norfeldt Elementary School
West Hartford, CT

Child-Centered Conferencing

Description

Our goal is to assist students, parents, and teachers in creating a successful child-centered program that guarantees new achievement levels for all students.

The child moves to full center of this program, fully participating in three conferences with parents and the teacher. Together they assess skills, set goals, and focus on self-esteem.

Teachers prepare a student education plan for each child. This is a portfolio that includes samples of work (some to keep at home and some for permanent filing), along with a comprehensive assessment form that emphasizes production and responsibility.

Benefits

There is a great deal of excitement on our campus about how students are responding to the education plan and the conferencing model. When young people are empowered to develop new skills, to evaluate goals, and to make responsible decisions, they lengthen their strides toward becoming responsible citizens.

Parents accept fuller responsibility as well. Not only does a child's increased participation with adults ensure greater student involvement and understanding but the plan also offers parents new insights into their children and the process of teacher accountability.

Velda S. Morrow, Principal
George Q. Knowlton Elementary School
Farmington, UT

Extended Day

Description

We have extended our school day by offering after-school clubs to provide children with dynamic learning opportunities that are difficult to duplicate during the school day. The clubs most exciting to students are gardening, computers, drama, clown college, pottery, math, magic, chorus, printing, French, Spanish, science olympiad, and folk dancing, to name a few.

Clubs usually meet 1 hour twice a week for 3 weeks in classrooms, the media center, the outdoors, or the auditorium. Children are charged a $10.00 fee that pays for consultants and materials, but anyone may attend, so that money is no obstacle.

Benefits

The clubs are extremely popular with students. We have close to a 70% participation rate.

Dr. John E. Bley, Principal
Kathie W. Dobberteen, Former Principal
Glenn E. Murdock Elementary School
La Mesa, CA

Academic Best

Description

Our principal sponsors a monthly schoolwide display of academic excellence. The goal is to have each child achieve this honor at least once during the year. In actuality, about 90% of our students meet the goal.

Teachers select a sample of a student's best work and submit it to the principal's office. Each month, students whose work is chosen are presented an "Academic Excellence" pin and have their names read over the intercom.

Benefits

Students respond positively to acknowledgment from their school family for their best efforts. However, the most significant recognition is a personalized letter to the child's parents. This letter is always mailed home on a Friday morning so that it will arrive on Saturday.

Robert Gaines, Principal
Caroline Bentley School
New Lenox, IL

Just Say "Hello"

Description

An important component of our school day is the emphasis on building positive relationships, the foundation of academic and personal growth. Maintaining a positive attitude is a primary objective of teachers, whether they are in the classrooms or hallways, or are leading extracurricular activities.

During the school day, the teachers greet students and have a brief, supportive interchange as frequently as possible. The principal says, "Hello," as children arrive for school each morning. Of course, doing this job well requires both a sincere attempt to learn the names of all students and a commitment to be consistent—rain or shine.

Benefits

Students feel they personally know teachers and the principal, and they are personally known, in a constructive way. The daily greeting has been positive, especially for students who have difficulty in accomplishing schoolwork or in maintaining high behavioral standards.

There is a fringe benefit. It is a great lift for the teachers and principal, too!

Reed S. Sander, Principal
Trinity Lutheran School
Roselle, IL

A blue-ribbon scholar.

1991-1992 Blue Ribbon Elementary and Middle Schools

ALABAMA

Edgewood Elementary School
901 College Avenue
Homewood, AL 35209
(205) 942-8607

Eura Brown Elementary School
1231 Alcott Road
Gadsden, AL 35901
(205) 546-0011

Grantswood Community School
Route 4, Box 858
Grantswood Road
Irondale, AL 35210
(205) 956-5663

Pinson Elementary School
4200 School Drive
Pinson, AL 35126
(205) 681-7021

ARIZONA

Craycroft Elementary School
5455 E. Littletown Road
Tucson, AZ 85706-9400
(602) 741-2405

Sandpiper Elementary School
6724 East Hearn
Scottsdale, AZ 85254
(602) 493-6210

Sequoya Elementary School
11808 North 64th Street
Scottsdale, AZ 85254
(602) 443-7860

Show Low Primary School
1350 North Central
Show Low, AZ 85901
(602) 537-4525

ARKANSAS

Root Elementary School
1529 Mission
Fayetteville, AR 72701
(501) 444-3075

CALIFORNIA

Alamo Elementary School
100 Wilson Road
Alamo, CA 94507
(510) 938-0448

Brywood Elementary School
#1 Westwood
Irvine, CA 92720
(714) 857-9230

Bullis-Purissima School
25890 Fremont Road
Los Altos Hills, CA 94022
(415) 941-3880

Chaparral Elementary School
17250 Tannin Drive
Poway, CA 92064
(619) 485-0042

Charles E. Teach Elementary
School
375 Ferrini Road
San Luis Obispo, CA 93405
(805) 546-9355

Foothill Elementary School
13919 Lynde Avenue
Saratoga, CA 95070
(408) 867-4036

Fort Washington Elementary
School
960 East Teague
Fresno, CA 93720
(209) 439-0520

Glenn E. Murdock Elementary
School
4354 Conrad Drive
La Mesa, CA 91941
(619) 668-5775

Graystone Elementary School
6982 Shearwater Drive
San Jose, CA 95120
(408) 998-6317

Mayfield Junior School of the
Holy Child
P.O. Box 90457
Pasadena, CA 91109-0457
(818) 796-2774

Monte Gardens Elementary School
3841 Larkspur Drive
Concord, CA 94519
(510) 685-3834

Nelson Elementary School
1336 W. Spruce Avenue
Pinedale, CA 93650
(209) 439-0176

Oak Hills Elementary School
1010 Kanan Road
Agoura, CA 91301
(818) 707-4224

Oakbrook Elementary School
700 Oakbrook Drive
Fairfield, CA 94585
(707) 421-4205

Quailwood Elementary School
7301 Remington Avenue
Bakersfield, CA 93309
(805) 832-6415

Rio Vista Elementary School
20417 Cedarcreek Street
Canyon Country, CA 91351
(805) 297-8880

R. J. Neutra Elementary School
P.O. Box 1339 - Hawkeye &
Oriskany
NAS Lemoore, CA 93245
(209) 998-6823

Saint Simon School
1840 Grant Road
Los Altos, CA 94024
(415) 968-9952

San Diego Hebrew Day School
6365 Lake Atlin Avenue
San Diego, CA 92119
(619) 460-3300

Santa Rita Elementary School
700 Los Altos Avenue
Los Altos, CA 94022
(415) 941-3288

St. Thomas the Apostle School
2632 West 15th Street
Los Angeles, CA 90006
(213) 737-4730

Village Elementary School
900 Yulupa Avenue
Santa Rosa, CA 95405
(707) 545-5754

Willow Elementary School
29026 Laro Drive
Agoura Hills, CA 91301
(818) 889-0677

COLORADO

Pioneer Elementary School
3663 Woodland Hills Drive
Colorado Springs, CO 80918
(719) 598-8232

St. Mary's Academy
4545 S. University Boulevard
Englewood, CO 80110-6099
(303) 762-8300

CONNECTICUT

Eastern Middle School
51 Hendrie Avenue
Riverside, CT 06878
(203) 637-1744

Eric G. Norfeldt Elementary
School
35 Barksdale Road
West Hartford, CT 06117
(203) 233-4421

Mansfield Middle School
205 Spring Hill Road
Storrs, CT 06268
(203) 429-9341

Northeast Elementary School
71 East Street
Vernon, CT 06066
(203) 875-5751

Union School
173 School Street
Unionville, CT 06085
(203) 673-2575

DELAWARE

St. Matthew School
1 Fallon Avenue, Woodcrest
Wilmington, DE 19804-1998
(302) 633-5860

DISTRICT OF COLUMBIA

Bunker Hill Community School
14th and Michigan Avenue N.E.
Washington, DC 20017
(202) 576-6095

FLORIDA

Cushman School
592 Northeast 60 Street
Miami, FL 33137
(305) 757-1966

Griffin Elementary School
5050 S.W. 116th Avenue
Cooper City, FL 33330
(305) 680-1070

Gulliver Academy
12595 Red Road
Coral Gables, FL 33156
(305) 665-3593

Heights Elementary School
15200 Alexandria Court
Fort Myers, FL 33908
(813) 481-1761

N. B. Broward Elementary School
400 West Osborne Avenue
Tampa, FL 33603
(813) 276-5592

Nob Hill Elementary School
2100 Northwest 104 Avenue
Sunrise, FL 33322
(305) 572-1240

North Dade Center for Modern
Languages
1840 Northwest 157 Street
Miami, FL 33054
(305) 625-3885

Oak Hill Elementary School
6910 Daughtry Boulevard South
Jacksonville, FL 32210
(904) 573-1031

Sanibel Elementary School
3840 Sanibel Captiva Road
Sanibel, FL 33957
(813) 472-1617

Thomas Jefferson Middle School
525 N.W. 147th Street
Miami, FL 33168
(305) 681-7481

Westchester Elementary School
12405 Royal Palm Boulevard
Coral Springs, FL 33065
(305) 344-2380

GEORGIA

A. L. Burruss Elementary School
325 Manning Road
Marietta, GA 30064
(404) 428-3417

Cook Middle School
310 North Martin Luther King
Drive
Adel, GA 31620
(912) 896-4541

Graysville Elementary School
Box 10
Graysville, GA 30726
(706) 937-3147

McCleskey Middle School
4080 Maybreeze Road
Marietta, GA 30066
(404) 591-6841

Pinckneyville Middle School
5440 W. Jones Bridge Road
Norcross, GA 30092
(404) 263-0860

R. D. Head Elementary School
1801 Hewatt Road
Lilburn, GA 30247
(404) 972-8050

Savannah Country Day School
824 Stillwood Drive
Savannah, GA 31419-2643
(912) 925-8800

St. Marys Elementary School
510 Osborne Street
St. Marys, GA 31558
(912) 882-4839 or -4425

HAWAII

ASSETS School
Box 106
Building 281, 286, 287
Honolulu, HI 96860
(808) 423-1356

Kapunahala Elementary School
45-828 Anoi Road
Kaneohe, HI 96744
(808) 247-1011

Mililani-uka Elementary School
94-380 Kuahelani Avenue
Mililani, HI 96789
(808) 623-3077

Princess Miriam K. Likelike
Elementary School
1618 Palama Street
Honolulu, HI 96817
(808) 845-4123

ILLINOIS

Adler Park School
1740 N. Milwaukee Avenue
Libertyville, IL 60048
(708) 362-7275

Arnold J. Tyler School
501 E. Illinois Highway
New Lenox, IL 60451
(815) 485-2398

Caroline Bentley School
511 E. Illinois Highway
New Lenox, IL 60451
(815) 485-4451

Grove Avenue School
900 Grove Avenue
Barrington, IL 60010
(708) 381-1888

Lake Bluff Junior High School
31 E. Sheridan Place
Lake Bluff, IL 60044
(708) 234-9407

Laura B. Sprague School
2425 Riverwoods Road
Lincolnshire, IL 60069
(708) 945-6665

Northbrook Junior High School
1475 Maple Avenue
Northbrook, IL 60062
(708) 498-7920

Sheridan School
1360 Sheridan Road
Lake Forest, IL 60045
(708) 234-1160

St. Damian School
5300 W. 155th Street
Oak Forest, IL 60452-3358
(708) 687-4230

St. Luke School
519 Ashland Avenue
River Forest, IL 60305
(708) 366-8587

Trinity Lutheran School
405 South Rush Street
Roselle, IL 60172-2294
(708) 894-3263

Washington School
122 S. Garfield
Mundelein, IL 60060
(708) 949-2714

INDIANA

Brumfield Elementary School
R.R. 3, Old Highway 41 North
Princeton, IN 47670
(812) 386-1221

Edward Eggleston Elementary
School
19010 Adams Road
South Bend, IN 46637
(219) 272-4311

Harold Handley Elementary
School
408 W. Tenth Street
LaPorte, IN 46350
(219) 362-2561

Klondike Elementary School
3311 Klondike Road
W. Lafayette, IN 47906
(317) 463-5505

IOWA

CAL Elementary School
P.O. Box 459
Latimer, IA 50452
(515) 579-6085

Grant Wood Elementary School
645—26th Street SE
Cedar Rapids, IA 52403
(319) 398-2467

Regina Elementary School
2120 Rochester Avenue
Iowa City, IA 52245
(319) 337-5739

KANSAS

Countryside Elementary School
15800 W. 124th Terrace
Olathe, KS 66062
(913) 780-7390

Indian Creek Elementary School
15800 W. Indian Creek Parkway
Olathe, KS 66062
(913) 780-7510

Leawood Elementary School
2400 West 123rd Street
Leawood, KS 66209
(913) 345-7425

Oak Hill Elementary School
10200 West 124th Street
Overland Park, KS 66213
(913) 681-4325

Oxford Middle School
12500 Switzer
Overland Park, KS 66213
(913) 681-4175

KENTUCKY

Marshall Elementary School
Texas at 29th Street
Fort Campbell, KY 42223-5000
(502) 439-7766

Robert D. Johnson Elementary
School
1180 North Fort Thomas Avenue
Fort Thomas, KY 41075
(606) 441-2444

Virginia Wheeler Elementary
School
5410 Cynthia Drive
Louisville, KY 40291
(502) 473-8349

LOUISIANA

Gentilly Terrace Creative Arts
Magnet School
4720 Painters Street
New Orleans, LA 70122
(504) 286-2670

Saint Rosalie School
617 Second Avenue
Harvey, LA 70058
(504) 341-4342

MAINE

Biddeford Middle School
335 Hill Street
Biddeford, ME 04005
(207) 282-5957

Bowdoin Central School
R.F.D. #2, Box 3744
Bowdoinham, ME 04008
(207) 666-5779

Howard C. Reiche Community
School
166 Brackett Street
Portland, ME 04102
(207) 874-8175

MARYLAND

Candlewood Elementary School
7210 Osprey Drive
Rockville, MD 20855
(301) 840-7167

Frances R. Fuchs Special Center
11011 Cherry Hill Road
Beltsville, MD 20705
(301) 937-5818

Greenbelt Center Elementary
School
15 Crescent Road
Greenbelt, MD 20770
(301) 474-7111

Lake Seneca Elementary School
13600 Wanegarden Drive
Germantown, MD 20874
(301) 353-0929

MASSACHUSETTS

Advent School
17 Brimmer Street
Boston, MA 02108
(617) 742-0520

Fay School
48 Main Street
P.O. Box 9106
Southborough, MA 01772-9106
(508) 485-0100

Henry C. Sanborn Elementary
School
Lovejoy Road
Andover, MA 01810
(508) 475-1393

Lighthouse School, Inc.
84 Billerica Road
Chelmsford, MA 01824
(508) 256-9300

MICHIGAN

Carl H. Lindbom Elementary
School
1010 State Street
Brighton, MI 48116
(313) 229-1477

Eastover Elementary School
1101 Westview Road
Bloomfield Hills, MI 48304
(313) 645-4550

Grosse Pointe Academy
171 Lake Shore Road
Grosse Pointe Farms, MI 48236
(313) 886-1221

Harlan Elementary School
3595 N. Adams Road
Bloomfield Hills, MI 48304
(313) 645-5750

Southwest Elementary School
915 Gay Street
Howell, MI 48843
(517) 548-6288

MINNESOTA

Clear Springs Elementary School
5701 Highway 101
Minnetonka, MN 55345
(612) 934-3993

Deephaven Elementary School
4452 Vine Hill Road
Wayzata, MN 55391
(612) 474-5448

Groves Learning Center
3200 Highway 100 South
St. Louis Park, MN 55416
(612) 920-6377

Highland Elementary School
14001 Pilot Knob Road
Apple Valley, MN 55124
(612) 423-7595

Hosterman Middle School
5530 Zealand Avenue North
New Hope, MN 55428
(612) 533-2411

Mounds Park Academy - Lower
School
2051 East Larpenteur Avenue
St. Paul, MN 55109-4785
(612) 777-2555

Susan Lindgren Intermediate
Center
4801 W. 41st Street
St. Louis Park, MN 55416-3245
(612) 922-1600

MISSOURI

Bellerive Elementary School
666 Rue de Fleur
Creve Coeur, MO 63141
(314) 878-3314

James Lewis Elementary School
717 Park Road
Blue Springs, MO 64015
(816) 224-1345

Knob Noster Elementary School
405 East Wimer Street
Knob Noster, MO 65336
(816) 563-3019

Midway Heights Elementary
School
8130 West Highway 40
Columbia, MO 65202
(314) 886-2380

Old Bonhomme Elementary
School
9661 Old Bonhomme Road
Olivette, MO 63132
(314) 993-0656

River Bend Elementary School
224 River Valley Drive
Chesterfield, MO 63017
(314) 469-7500

MONTANA

Havre Middle School
1441 11th Street West
Havre, MT 59501
(406) 265-9613

NEBRASKA

Longfellow Elementary School
2003 5th Avenue
Scottsbluff, NE 69361
(308) 635-6262

NEVADA

Brown Elementary School
13815 Spelling Court
Reno, NV 89511-7238
(702) 851-5600

Vegas Verdes Elementary School
4000 El Parque Avenue
Las Vegas, NV 89102
(702) 799-5960

NEW JERSEY

Canfield Avenue School
Canfield Avenue
Mine Hill, NJ 07801
(201) 366-0590

Eden Institute
1 Logan Drive
Princeton, NJ 08540
(609) 987-0099

George C. Baker Elementary
School
139 W. Maple Avenue
Moorestown, NJ 08057
(609) 235-4000

Greenbrook School
Roberts Street
Kendall Park, NJ 08824
(908) 297-2480

Lawrence Brook School
48 Sullivan Way
East Brunswick, NJ 08816
(908) 613-6870

Leesburg School
P.O. Box D
Port Elizabeth, NJ 08348
(609) 825-7411

Mill Lake School
Monmouth Road
Spotswood, NJ 08884
(908) 251-5336

Moorestown Friends Lower School
110 E. Main Street
Moorestown, NJ 08075
(609) 235-2913

NEW MEXICO

Loma Heights Elementary School
1600 E. Madrid Road
Las Cruces, NM 88001
(505) 527-9546

NEW YORK

Como Park Elementary School
1985 Como Park Boulevard
Lancaster, NY 14086
(716) 684-3235

Concord Road Elementary School
Concord Road
Ardsley, NY 10502
(914) 693-7510

Davison Avenue School
Davison Avenue
Lynbrook, NY 11563
(516) 596-2063

Herbert Hoover Elementary
School
199 Thorncliff Road
Kenmore, NY 14223
(716) 874-8414

Lake George Elementary School
RR #3, Box 3001
Lake George, NY 12845-9503
(518) 668-5714

Osborn School
Osborn Road
Rye, NY 10580
(914) 967-6100, Ext. 289

PEARLS Elementary School #32
Montclair & Dexter Road
Yonkers, NY 10710
(914) 376-8595

Salanter Akiba Riverdale Academy
655 West 254 Street
Riverdale, NY 10471
(212) 549-5160

Shelter Rock Elementary School
Shelter Rock Road
Manhasset, NY 11030
(516) 627-8120

Voorheesville Elementary School
Route 85A
Voorheesville, NY 12186
(518) 765-2382

Wantagh Elementary School
1765 Beech Street
Wantagh, NY 11793
(516) 781-2970

NORTH CAROLINA

Lewis H. Powell Gifted and
Talented Magnet Elementary
School
1130 Marlborough Road
Raleigh, NC 27610
(919) 856-7737

NORTH DAKOTA

Belmont Elementary School
407 Chestnut Street
Grand Forks, ND 58201
(701) 746-2240

Clara Barton Elementary School
1417 Sixth Street South
Fargo, ND 58103
(701) 241-4761

OHIO

Bellflower Elementary School
6655 Reynolds Road
Mentor, OH 44060
(216) 255-4212

Canton Country Day School
3000 Demington Avenue, N.W.
Canton, OH 44718
(216) 453-8279

Freedom Elementary School
6035 Beckett Ridge Boulevard
West Chester, OH 45069
(513) 777-9787

Hoffman School
3060 Durrell Avenue
Cincinnati, OH 45207
(513) 872-7230

Hopewell Elementary School
8300 Cox Road
West Chester, OH 45069
(513) 777-6128

Kilgour Elementary School
1339 Herschel Avenue
Cincinnati, OH 45208
(513) 321-7840

Lial Elementary School
5900 Davis Road
Whitehouse, OH 43571
(419) 877-5167

Normandy Elementary School
401 Normandy Ridge Road
Centerville, OH 45459
(513) 434-0917

Our Lady of Perpetual Help
School
3752 Broadway
Grove City, OH 43123
(614) 875-6779

Pine Elementary School
4267 Dover Center Road
North Olmsted, OH 44070
(216) 779-3536

Sharonville Elementary School
11150 Maple Street
Cincinnati, OH 45241
(513) 563-6393

St. Andrew School
4081 Reed Road
Columbus, OH 43220
(614) 451-1626

St. James White Oak School
6111 Cheviot Road
Cincinnati, OH 45247
(513) 741-5333

St. John Bosco School
6460 Pearl Road
Parma Heights, OH 44130
(216) 886-0061

OKLAHOMA

Quail Creek Elementary School
11700 Thorn Ridge Road
Oklahoma City, OK 73120
(405) 751-3231

OREGON

Slater/Filmore Grade School
800 North Fairview Avenue
Burns, OR 97720
(503) 573-7201

Washington Elementary School
610 Peach Street
Medford, OR 97501
(503) 776-8860

PENNSYLVANIA

Ancillae-Ascumpta Academy
2025 Church Road
Wyncote, PA 19095
(215) 885-1636

Boyce Middle School
1500 Boyce Road
Upper St. Clair, PA 15241
(412) 854-3043

Cynwyd Elementary School
101 W. Levering Mill Road
Bala Cynwyd, PA 19004
(215) 664-5091

Dorothea H. Simmons School
411 Babylon Road
Horsham, PA 19002
(215) 956-2929

John M. Grasse Elementary School
600 Rickert Road
Sellersville, PA 18960
(215) 723-7501

O'Hara Elementary School
115 Cabin Lane
Pittsburgh, PA 15238
(412) 963-0333

Swarthmore Rutledge School
100 College Avenue
Swarthmore, PA 19081
(215) 544-5700

PUERTO RICO

Colegio Ponceno
Ponce, Puerto Rico 00780-9508
(809) 848-2525

Francisco Matias Lugo School
Calle Almendro
Valle Arriba Heights
Carolina, Puerto Rico 00984
(809) 757-0410

RHODE ISLAND

Dr. James H. Eldredge Elementary
School
145 First Avenue
East Greenwich, RI 02818
(401) 885-3300

SOUTH CAROLINA

Ashley River Creative Arts
Elementary School
1871 Wallace School Road
Charleston, SC 29407
(803) 763-1555

Baker's Chapel Elementary School
555 South Old Piedmont Highway
Greenville, SC 29611-6141
(803) 299-8320

TENNESSEE

Brookmeade Elementary School
1015 Davidson Drive
Nashville, TN 37205
(615) 353-2000

Glendale Middle School
800 Thompson Avenue
Nashville, TN 37204
(615) 298-8077

Sacred Heart Cathedral School
711 Northshore Drive
Knoxville, TN 37919
(615) 588-0415

Whiteville Elementary School
P.O. Box 659 - Highway 100
Bypass
Whiteville, TN 38075
(901) 254-8013 or -8561

TEXAS

All Saints Episcopal School
P.O. Box 64545
Lubbock, TX 79464
(806) 745-7701

Bunker Hill Elementary School
11950 Taylorcrest
Houston, TX 77024
(713) 465-0036

Christa McAuliffe Elementary
School
2300 Briarhill Boulevard
Lewisville, TX 75067
(214) 221-9909

Francone Elementary School
11250 Perry Road
Houston, TX 77064
(713) 897-4512

Good Shepherd Episcopal School
11122 Midway Road
Dallas, TX 75229
(214) 357-1610

Highland Park Elementary School
4900 Fairview Drive
Austin, TX 78731
(512) 459-6313

Huffman Elementary School
5510 Channel Isle Drive
Plano, TX 75093
(214) 248-1818

Kimberlin Academy for Excellence
1520 Cumberland Drive
Garland, TX 75040
(214) 494-8365

Laurel Mountain Elementary
School
10111 D K Ranch Road
Austin, TX 78759
(512) 258-1373

Live Oak Elementary School
8607 Anderson Mill Road
Austin, TX 78729-4706
(512) 331-0996

Lowery Elementary School
15950 Ridge Park
Houston, TX 77095
(713) 463-5900

L. P. Montgomery Elementary
School
2807 Amber Lane
Farmers Branch, TX 75234
(214) 241-2594

Mirabeau B. Lamar Elementary
School
2212 Morris Street
Corpus Christi, TX 78405
(512) 886-9321

Nottingham Elementary School
570 Nottingham Oaks Trail
Houston, TX 77079
(713) 497-2954

River Oaks Baptist School
2300 Willowick Street
Houston, TX 77027
(713) 623-6938

Robert E. Lee Elementary School
3308 Hampton Road
Austin, TX 78703
(512) 478-2711

Robert S. Hyer Elementary School
3920 Caruth Boulevard
Dallas, TX 75225
(214) 361-5656

Saigling Elementary School
3600 Matterhorn Drive
Plano, TX 75075
(214) 596-2300

Shepard Elementary School
1000 Wilson Drive
Plano, TX 75075
(214) 423-8001

St. James Episcopal School
602 S. Carancahua Street
Corpus Christi, TX 78401
(512) 883-0835

St. Mark the Evangelist Catholic
School
1201 Alma Drive
Plano, TX 75075
(214) 578-0610

Tanglewood Elementary School
3060 Overton Park Drive W.
Fort Worth, TX 76109
(817) 922-6819

T. F. Birmingham Elementary
School
700 West Brown Street
Wylie, TX 75098
(214) 442-6512

T. H. Rogers School
5840 San Felipe
Houston, TX 77057
(713) 783-6220

W.H.L. Wells Elementary School
3427 Mission Ridge
Plano, TX 75023
(214) 596-3618

UTAH

George Q. Knowlton Elementary
School
801 West Shepard Lane
Farmington, UT 84025
(801) 451-1045

VERMONT

Chamberlin School
262 White Street
South Burlington, VT 05403
(802) 658-9040

Richmond Elementary School
RR 1, Box 551
Jericho Road
Richmond, VT 05477
(802) 434-2461

VIRGIN ISLANDS

Antilles School
P.O. Box 7280
St. Thomas, Virgin Islands 00801
(809) 774-1966

VIRGINIA

Highland Park Learning Center
Magnet School
1212 Fifth Street, SW
Roanoke, VA 24012
(703) 981-2963

Rawls Byrd Elementary School
112 Laurel Lane
Williamsburg, VA 23185
(804) 229-7597

WASHINGTON

Eton School
2701 Bel-Red Road
Bellevue, WA 98008-2253
(206) 881-4230

Hazelwood Elementary School
6928 116th Avenue S.E.
Renton, WA 98056
(206) 235-2283

Skyline Elementary School
2225 Thornton Street
Ferndale, WA 98248-0905
(206) 384-9245

Spring Glen Elementary School
2607 Jones Avenue South
Renton, WA 98055
(206) 859-7494

St. Philomena Catholic School
1815 South 220th
Des Moines, WA 98198
(206) 824-4051

WEST VIRGINIA

Elm Grove Elementary School
R.D. #2, Box 444
Wheeling, WV 26003
(304) 243-0363

High Lawn Elementary School
2400 Kanawha Terrace
St. Albans, WV 25177
(304) 722-0220

Our Lady of Fatima School
535 Norway Avenue
Huntington, WV 25705
(304) 523-2861

Tiskelwah Elementary School
600 Florida Street
Charleston, WV 25302
(304) 348-6622

WISCONSIN

Crestwood Elementary School
5930 Old Sauk Road
Madison, WI 53705
(608) 231-4550

Jefferson Elementary School
105 Ice Street
Menasha, WI 54952
(414) 751-5093

John Muir Elementary School
6602 Inner Drive
Madison, WI 53705
(608) 829-4130

St. Paul's Lutheran School
210 South Ringold Street
Janesville, WI 53545
(608) 754-4471

WYOMING

Crest Hill Elementary School
4445 South Poplar
Casper, WY 82716
(307) 577-4512

OVERSEAS

Coevorden American School
Unit 6840
APO AE 09719
(011) 31-5240-17923

Please feel free to use this list to network with these Blue Ribbon Schools. For more information on the Blue Ribbon Schools Program for elementary, middle, and secondary schools, please contact the following:

Blue Ribbon Schools Program
Office of Educational Research and Improvement (OERI)
U.S. Department of Education
Washington, DC 20208-5645
(202) 219-2149

or for elementary and middle schools only:

National Association of Elementary School Principals
Special Projects Division
1615 Duke Street
Alexandria, Virginia 22314-3483
(703) 684-3345